H

Se… …dited by
Geoff Barton

Oxford University Press

Oxford University Press, Walton Street, Oxford OX2 6DP

Oxford New York Toronto
Delhi Bombay Calcutta Madras Karachi
Kuala Lumpur Singapore Hong Kong Tokyo
Nairobi Dar es Salaam Cape Town
Melbourne Auckland Madrid

and associated companies in
Berlin Ibadan

Oxford is a trade mark of Oxford University Press

ISBN 0 19 831284 9

Typeset by Pentacor PLC, High Wycombe, Bucks
Printed and Bound in Great Britain

Cover illustration by Gwyn Hughes/Allied Artists

Also available in the *Oxford Literature Resources* series:

Contemporary Stories 1	0 19 831251 2
Contemporary Stories 2	0 19 831254 7
Stories from South Asia	0 19 831255 5
Science Fiction Stories	0 19 831261 X
Fantasy Stories	0 19 831262 8
Sport	0 19 831264 4
Autobiography	0 19 831265 2
Love	0 19 831279 2
Crime Stories	0 19 831280 6
Scottish Short Stories	0 19 831281 4
American Short Stories	0 19 831282 2
Travel Writing	0 19 831283 0

Contents

Acknowledgements

The editor and publisher are grateful for permission to include the following copyright material in this collection.

Jan Arriens: for letters from *Welcome to Hell*, edited by Jan Arriens, (Faulkner, 1991). **The British Broadcasting Corporation**, John Simpson and Paul Hamann: for extracts from *The Nine O'Clock News*, BBC1 26.10.92, © BBC 1992, and *Fourteen Days in May*, BBC1 11.11.87, © BBC 1987. **Curtis Brown Ltd**, London, on behalf of the Mass-Observation Archive at the University of Sussex: for extract from *Speak for Yourself: A Mass-Observation Anthology, 1937-49* edited by Angus Calder and Dorothy Sheridan (Cape, 1984), Copyright the Trustees of the Mass-Observation Archive. **Paul Buttle**, Picture Editor, *The Sun*: for his letter. **Express** Newspapers: for article by Antonia Swinson, 'Where the Law is not Blind to Colour', *The Daily Express*, 12.11.87. **Endeavor**/Robert West: for letter in *Endeavor: Live Voices from Death Row Across the USA*. Vol.1:1, 1989. **The Guardian**: for abridged article by John Diamond, © The Guardian, 1992. **Nick Hern Books**, 14 Larden Road, London W3 7ST: for excerpts from Arthur Miller's adaptation of Ibsen's *An Enemy of the People*, copyright © 1950, 1951, 1989. **Richard Joseph Publishers Ltd**: for extract of introduction by John Frost to Brian Lake (ed): *British Newspapers: A History and Guide for Collectors*, (Sheppard, 1984). **Longman Group UK**: for *The Wheatley Diary*, edited by Christopher Hibbert, (1961). **Hilary Minns**: for figures from *Language, Literacy and Gender* (Hodder & Stoughton, 1991). **Kenneth Morgan**, former Director of The Press Council (now the Press Complaints Commission): for his letter. **Thomas Nelson & Sons Ltd**: for transcript of interview with Kate Adie from *Initiatives: Reportage* (1989). **Newspaper Publishing plc**: for editorial 'Up and Down the City Road' by The Weasel, *Independent Magazine*. 15.8.92, and articles by William Leith, 'What do you Get if you Cross a Chicken with a Rottweiler', *Independent on Sunday*, 17.5.92, by Phil Reeves and David Usborne, 'Plop, Plop, Fizz, Fizz' *Independent on Sunday*, 26.4.92, and by Thomas Sutcliffe, 'Chronicle of a Death Foretold' *Independent*, 12.11.87. **The Observer**: for extracts from *The Observer*, from *The Observer Observed* by Joanna Anstey and John Silverlight, *The Observer* © (Barrie & Jenkins, 1991). **Pavilion Books Ltd**: for extracts from *How It Was In the War* edited by Godfrey Smith,

(1989). **Penguin Books Ltd**: for extract from *The Letters of the Younger Pliny*, translated by Betty Radice (Penguin Classics, 1963) copyright © Betty Radice, 1963, 1967. **Peters Frazer & Dunlop Group Ltd**: for extract from introduction by Tom Wolfe to *The New Journalism: Law and Lawlessness*, (Picador, 1990). **Picador**, a Division of Pan Macmillan Ltd: for extract from *Republican Party Reptile* by P.J. O'Rourke, (1987). **Random Century Group**: for extract from *Unreasonable Behaviour: An Autobiography* by Don McCullin, (Jonathan Cape, 1990), and on behalf of the Estate of the author for extract from *Warrior Without Weapons* by Marcel Junod, translated by Edward Fitzgerald, (Jonathan Cape, 1951). **Random House Inc. and International Creative Management Inc**: for extract from 'What I Saw at the Revolution' by Peggy Noonan, copyright © 1989 Peggy Noonan. **Reed International Books**: for extract from *Stick It Up Your Punter! The Fall and Rise of the "Sun"* by Peter Chippendale & Chris Horrie, (Heinemann, 1992), and for extract from *Among the Thugs*, by Bill Buford, (Secker & Warburg, 1991). **Rogers Coleridge & White**: for extract from *Lies, Damned Lies, and A Few Exclusives* by Henry Porter, (Chatto & Windus, 1984). **Sharon and Zoë** for their letter to the Press Council. **Sidgwick & Jackson**: for extract from *Is That It?* by Bob Geldof, (Sidgwick, 1986).

Although every effort has been made to trace and contact copyright holders prior to publication, this has not always been possible. If notified, the publisher will be pleased to rectify any errors or omissions at the earliest opportunity.

The publishers wish to thank the following for permission to reproduce photographs:

p.122 *top* Zydowski Institute, *bottom* Canapress Photo Service; p.123 Hulton Deutsch Collection; p.124 *top* Topham Picture Source, *bottom* Associated Press; p.125 Press Association; p.126 Tony McGrath/The Observer; p.127 Steve Ringman/San Francisco Chronicle.

Preface

Reportage is more than an anthology of journalism. It is concerned with the *process* of reporting in various media: newspaper stories are one important part of this process. The book starts with a series of eyewitness accounts never intended for publication in newspapers or magazines. How do ordinary people respond on the spot to dramatic events such as disasters and wars? Often their first impressions, noted in diaries, journals, and letters, capture unexpected events with astonishing intensity and immediacy. Their responses often represent the first stage in the reporting process, even though the writers often have no specific sense of audience in mind.

The journalist's role is different. He or she is likely to be sent to an event with instructions to cover it on behalf of readers, listeners or viewers who are far removed from the action. This sense of writing for an audience makes the journalist's role distinct from that of the eyewitness, and this contrast is explored in the book. As a result, similar events are frequently presented from different angles by writers whose purposes are very different. What then are the challenges of being a journalist, and what are the responsibilities? The second section of *Reportage*: Journalism and Journalists invites a critical look at journalists' work, in newspapers and the wider media.

The restrictions of conventional journalism – having to report 'objectively', for example – have led some writers to experiment with different forms. Using techniques borrowed from novelists, writers of 'new' journalism aim to convey events and impressions in a style which involves both writer and reader in a more active way. A number of such writers are represented in *Reportage* and readers are encouraged to explore the effects of their prose styles. Does a news story become less 'reliable' if the writer recreates some scenes from imagination? Or does all reportage involve some degree of storytelling?

Having looked at some examples of the different forms of journalism, the Special Assignment section presents a variety of approaches to a single, urgent issue: capital punishment. How do people face the death penalty? How do different media 'cover' the event? Newspaper reports, letters, eyewitness accounts, essays and documentary footage all focus on this important subject. It should enable readers to consider in greater depth how different modes of reportage provoke different responses from their audiences.

Finally, *Reportage* invites readers to examine the rights and wrongs of certain reporting techniques. Some writers describe their powerful responses to media events which have changed their lives; others argue strongly that the media abuses its position by exploiting people's lives and invading their privacy. Readers are encouraged to reflect upon their own standards in these matters, as the ethics of the media are placed under closer scrutiny.

Reflection, in fact, is the central theme of the book. All of the accompanying activities invite readers to put themselves in the position of eyewitness, journalist, documentary-producer, reader, viewer or critic, to experiment with a variety of reporting techniques, and to reflect upon the place and purpose of the media in our society.

I hope that your encounters with the variety of themes, issues and genres contained in *Reportage* lead you into some lively debates and result in some challenging assignments.

Geoff Barton

Eyewitnesses: Disasters and War

The Eruption of Vesuvius

Pliny the Younger

My uncle was stationed at Misenum, in active command of the fleet. On 24 August, in the early afternoon, my mother drew his attention to a cloud of unusual size and appearance. He had been out in the sun, had taken a cold bath, and lunched while lying down, and was then working at his books. He called for his shoes and climbed up to a place which would give him the best view of the phenomenon. It was not clear at that distance from which mountain the cloud was rising (it was afterwards known to be Vesuvius); its general appearance can best be expressed as being like an umbrella pine, for it rose to a great height on a sort of trunk and then split off into branches, I imagine because it was thrust upwards by the first blast and then left unsupported as the pressure subsided, or else it was borne down by its own weight so that it spread out and gradually dispersed. In places it looked white, elsewhere blotched and dirty, according to the amount of soil and ashes it carried with it. My uncle's scholarly acumen saw at once that it was important enough for a closer inspection, and he ordered a boat to be made ready, telling me I could come with him if I wished. I replied that I preferred to go on with my studies, and as it happened he had himself given me some writing to do.

As he was leaving the house he was handed a message from Rectina, wife of Tascus whose house was at the foot of the mountain, so that escape was impossible except by boat. She was terrified by the danger threatening her and implored him to rescue her from her fate. He changed his plans, and what he had begun in a spirit of inquiry he completed as a hero. He gave orders for the warships to be launched and went on board himself with the intention of bringing help to many more people besides Rectina, for this lovely stretch of coast was thickly populated. He hurried to the place which everyone else was hastily leaving, steering his course straight for the danger zone. He was entirely fearless, describing each new movement and phase of the portent to be noted down exactly as he observed them. Ashes were already falling, hotter and thicker as the ships drew near, followed by bits of pumice and blackened stones, charred and cracked by the flames: then suddenly they were in shallow water, and the shore was blocked by the debris from the mountain. For a moment my uncle wondered whether to turn back, but when the helmsman advised this he refused, telling him that Fortune stood by the courageous and they must make for Pomponianus at Stabiae. He was cut off there by the breadth of the bay (for the shore gradually curves round a basin filled by the sea) so that he was not as yet in danger, though it was clear that this would come nearer as it spread. Pomponianus had therefore already put his belongings on board ship, intending to escape if the contrary wind fell. This wind was of course full in my uncle's favour, and he was able to bring his ship in. He embraced his terrified friend, cheered and encouraged him, and thinking he could calm his fears by showing his own composure, gave orders that he was to be carried to the bathroom. After his bath he lay down and dined; he was quite cheerful, or at any rate he pretended he was, which was no less courageous.

Meanwhile on Mount Vesuvius broad sheets of fire and leaping flames blazed at several points, their bright glare emphasized by the darkness of night. My uncle tried to allay the fears of his companions by repeatedly declaring that these were nothing but bonfires left by the peasants in their terror, or else empty houses on fire in the districts they had abandoned. Then he went to rest and certainly slept, for as he was a stout man his breathing was rather loud and heavy and could be heard by people coming and going outside his door. By this time the courtyard giving access to his room was full of ashes mixed with pumice stones, so that its level had risen and if he had stayed in the room any longer he would never have got out. He was wakened, came out and joined Pomponianus and the rest of the household who had sat up all night. They debated whether to stay indoors or take their chance in the open, for the buildings were now shaking with violent shocks, and seemed to be swaying to and fro as if they were torn from their foundations. Outside, on the other hand, there was the danger of falling pumice stones, even though these were light and porous; however, after comparing the risks they chose the latter. In my uncle's case one reason outweighed the other, but for the others it was a choice of fears. As a protection against falling objects they put pillows on their heads tied down with cloths.

Elsewhere there was daylight by this time, but they were still in darkness, blacker and denser then any ordinary night, which they relieved by lighting torches and various kinds of lamp. My uncle decided to go down to the shore and investigate on the spot the possibility of any escape by sea, but he found the waves still wild and dangerous. A sheet was spread on the ground for him to lie down, and he repeatedly asked for cold water to drink. Then the flames and smell of sulphur which gave warning of the approaching fire drove the others to take flight and roused him to stand up. He stood leaning on two slaves and then suddenly collapsed, I imagine because the dense fumes choked his breathing by blocking his windpipe which was constitutionally weak and narrow and often inflamed. When daylight returned on the 26th – two days after the last day he had seen – his body was found intact and uninjured, still fully clothed and looking more like sleep than death.

Meanwhile my mother and I were at Misenum... After my uncle's departure I spent the rest of the day with my books, as this was my reason for staying behind. Then I took a bath, dined, and then dozed fitfully for a while. For several days past there had been earth tremors which were not particularly alarming because they are frequent in Campania: but that night the shocks were so violent that everything felt as if it were not only shaken but overturned. My mother hurried into my room and found me already getting up to wake her if she were still asleep. We sat down in the forecourt of the house, between the building and the sea close by. I don't know whether I should call this courage or folly on my part (I was only seventeen at the time) but I called for a volume of Livy and went on reading as if I had nothing else to do. I even went on with the extracts I had been making. Up came a friend of my uncle's who had just come from Spain to join him. When he saw us sitting there and me actually reading, he scolded us both – me for my foolhardiness and my mother for allowing it. Nevertheless, I remained absorbed in my book.

By now it was dawn, but the light was still dim and faint. The buildings round us were already tottering, and the open space we were in was too small for us not to be in real and imminent danger if the house collapsed. This finally decided us to leave the town. We were followed by a panic-stricken mob of people wanting to act on someone else's decision in preference to their own (a point in which fear looks like prudence), who hurried us on our way by pressing hard behind in a dense crowd. Once beyond the buildings we stopped, and there we had some extraordinary experiences which thoroughly alarmed us. The carriages we had ordered to be brought out began to run in different directions though the ground was quite level, and would not remain stationary even when wedged with stones. We also saw the sea sucked away and apparently forced back by the earthquake: at any rate it receded from the shore so that quantities of sea creatures were left stranded on dry sand. On the landward side a fearful black cloud was rent by forked and quivering bursts of flame, and parted to reveal great tongues of fire, like flashes of lightning magnified in size.

At this point my uncle's friend from Spain spoke up still more urgently, 'If your brother, if your uncle is still alive, he will want you both to be saved; if he is dead, he would want you to survive him – why put off your escape?' We replied that we would not think of considering our own safety as long as we were uncertain of his. Without waiting any longer, our friend rushed off and hurried out of danger as fast as he could.

Soon afterwards the cloud sank down to earth and covered the sea; it had already blotted out Capri and hidden the promontory of Misenum from sight. Then my mother implored, entreated and commanded me to escape as best I could – a young man might escape, whereas she was old and slow and could die in peace as long as she had not been the cause of my death too. I refused to save myself without her, and grasping her hand forced her to quicken her pace. She gave in reluctantly, blaming herself for delaying me. Ashes were already falling, not as yet very thickly. I looked round: a dense black cloud was coming up behind us, spreading over the earth like a flood. 'Let us leave the road while we can still see,' I said, 'or we shall be knocked down and trampled underfoot in the dark by the crowd behind.' We had scarcely sat down to rest when darkness fell, not the dark of a moonless or cloudy night, but as if the lamp had been put out in a closed room. You could hear the shrieks of women, the wailing of infants, and the shouting of men; some were calling their parents, others their children or their wives, trying to recognize them by their voices. People bewailed their own fate or that of their relatives, and there were some who prayed for death in their terror of dying. Many besought the aid of the gods, but still more imagined there were no gods left, and that the universe was plunged into eternal darkness for evermore. There were people, too, who added to the real perils by inventing fictitious dangers: some reported that part of Misenum had collapsed or another part was on fire, and though their tales were false they found others to believe them. A gleam of light returned, but we took this to be a warning of the approaching flames rather than daylight. However, the flames remained some distance off; then darkness came on once more and ashes began to fall again, this time in heavy showers. We rose from time to time and shook them off, otherwise we should have been buried and crushed beneath their weight. I could boast that not a groan or cry of fear escaped me in these perils, but I admit that I derived some poor consolation in my mortal lot from the belief that the whole world was dying with me and I with it.

At last the darkness thinned and dispersed like smoke or cloud; then there was genuine daylight, and the sun actually shone out, but yellowish as it is during an eclipse. We were terrified to see everything changed, buried deep in ashes like snowdrifts. We returned to Misenum where we attended to our physical needs as best we could, and then spent an anxious night alternating between hope and fear. Fear predominated, for the earthquakes when on, and several hysterical individuals made their own and other people's calamities seem ludicrous in comparison with their frightful predictions. But even then, in spite of the dangers we had been through and were still expecting, my mother and I had still no intention of leaving until we had news of my uncle...

24 August AD79

Explosion on Board Brunel's *Great Eastern* Steamship

George Augustus Sala

Launched in 1858, Isambard Kingdom Brunel's prototype for the liner, *Great Eastern*, was the largest ship in the world. Here, a passenger describes an explosion on board.

We had dined. It was six o'clock, and we were off Hastings, at about seven miles' distance from the shore. The majority of the passengers, having finished their repast, had gone on deck. The ladies had retired, and, as we conjectured, according to their usual custom, to their boudoir. The dining saloon was deserted, save by a small knot of joyous guests, all known to each other, who had gathered round the most popular of the directors, Mr Ingram. That gentleman, his hand on the shoulder of his young son, was listening, not apparently unpleased, to the eloquence of a friend, who was decanting on his merits while proposing his health. The glasses were charged; the orator's peroration had culminated; the revellers were upstanding; when – as if the fingers of a man's hand had come out against the cabin wall, and written, as in sand, that the Medes and Persians were at the gate, the verberation of a tremendous explosion was heard. The reverberation followed. Then came – to our ears, who were in the dining room – a tremendous crash, not hollow, as of thunder, but solid, as of objects that offered resistance. Then a sweeping, rolling, swooping, rumbling sound, as of cannon balls scudding along the deck above. Remember, I am only describing *now* my personal experience and sensations. The rumbling noise was followed by the smash of the dining saloon skylights, and the irruption of a mass of fragments of wood and iron, followed by a thick cloud of powdered glass, and then by coaldust. My garments are full of the first, my hair and eyebrows of the last, now. There was but one impulse, one question – to go on deck; to ask, 'What can it be?' To me, the crash was greater than the explosion; and I thought more of a collision, or of the fall of one of the huge yards, than of an explosion; but my next neighbour cried out, 'The boiler has burst!' On gaining the deck I could at first see nothing but billows of steam rolling towards us. Then along the deck I saw the engine hose rapidly drawn along, and in another moment dozens of men were seizing it and carrying it forward. The wind was blowing tolerably strong, and when the steam cleared away a little in my immediate vicinity, there came an eddying shower of splinters, fragments of gilt moulding, shreds of ornamental paper, and tatters of crimson curtains. Several gentlemen now exerted themselves in the most praiseworthy manner to get the passengers aft; the danger was evidently forward; a thick cloud of steam there concealed all objects; but there was smoke as well as vapour, and I thought the ship was on fire. As men and passengers came rushing by I heard ejaculations of 'Fire', 'The boilers', 'The donkey engine has burst'; but these were more matters of question and answer than evidences of terror. There seemed to be amazement and curiosity, but – among the passengers at least – not the slightest panic...

...The effects of the catastrophe soon became lamentably apparent. One by one, borne on the shoulders or in the arms of their comrades, or, in one or two cases, staggering past, came by the unfortunate men who had been scalded in the stokehole. The face of one was utterly without human semblance, and looked simply like a mass of raw beefsteak. Another was so horribly scalded about the groin, that the two hands might be laid in the raw cavity, and scraps of his woollen undergarments were mixed up with hanks of boiled flesh. Another I saw had his trousers scalded away from the mid-thigh; his two legs, bare from thigh to heel, were continuous scalds, the skin and flesh hanging here and there. As they raised another man, the flesh of his hands came away in the grasp of those who held him, and he looked as though he had two bloody gloves on. There were some cases of severe contusions, and cuts from fractured glass; but curiously enough, not one instance of broken limb. Some of the sufferers were hysterical, laughing and crying in a pitiable manner. When in the hospital, or sick bay, the agony of some was so intolerable that – all gently and soothingly as it was done – they had to be held down. The remedies applied were linseed oil and cotton wool, continuously renewed.

Descending to the lower deck, the scene irresistibly reminded one of the interior of the area of Covent Garden Theatre after the fire of 1856. The vast expanse between decks was one heap of fragments. You trod upon one vast sultry mass of ruin and desolation. The nests of sleeping berths, the corridors and staircases were all (save the main one) gone. The cabin which with two friends I had occupied no longer existed. With all in the same block it had been blown entirely away. A portmanteau belonging to your correspondent was subsequently recovered from the *débâcle*; but my two companions lost everything they possessed on board. Forward, in this lower deck, you saw the great, gaping pit, which had vomited forth the fruits of the 'collapse'. It was an infernal region, that horrible hole. The bed of the accursed 'jacket', with torn and jagged ends, was still visible. In the hole, were beams and girders, planks and rails, and gigantic steampipes twisted double like disused speaking trumpets. The huge iron plates at the root of the funnel were torn or crumpled up like writing paper. The great wrought-iron girders supporting the lower deck were curved and bent; the flooring of the deck itself was, in part, upheaved, and disclosed ominous gaps. The boilers had sustained no injury. Weeks' time and thousands of pounds in expenditure must be consumed ere the *Great Eastern*'s proprietors will be able to repair the damage done to her 'main cabin fittings'.

Neither ship – as a ship – nor paddles, nor screw, were injured. At first there was an expressed intention to put into the nearest haven; but this idea was abandoned, and the *Great Eastern* proceeded on her voyage to Portland.

12 September 1859

The *Titanic*: From a Lifeboat

Mrs D. H. Bishop

We did not begin to understand the situation till we were perhaps a mile or more away from the *Titanic*. Then we could see the rows of lights along the decks begin to slant gradually upwards from the bow. Very slowly the lines of light began to point downward at a greater and greater angle. The sinking was so slow that you could not perceive the lights of the deck changing their position. The slant seemed to be greater about every quarter of an hour. That was the only difference.

In a couple of hours, though, she began to go down more rapidly. Then the fearful sight began. The people in the ship were just beginning to realize how great their danger was. When the forward part of the ship dropped suddenly at a faster rate, so that the upward slope became marked, there was a sudden rush of passengers on all the decks towards the stern. It was like a wave. We could see the great black mass of people in the steerage sweeping to the rear part of the boat and breaking through into the upper decks. At the distance of about a mile we could distinguish everything through the night, which was perfectly clear. We could make out the increasing excitement on board the boat as the people, rushing to and fro, caused the deck lights to disappear and reappear as they passed in front of them.

This panic went on, it seemed, for an hour. Then suddenly the ship seemed to shoot up out of the water and stand there perpendicularly. It seemed to us that it stood upright in the water for four full minutes.

Then it began to slide gently downwards. Its speed increased as it went down head first, so that the stern shot down with a rush.

The lights continued to burn till it sank. We could see the people packed densely in the stern till it was gone...

...As the ship sank we could hear the screaming a mile away. Gradually it became fainter and fainter and died away. Some of the lifeboats that had room for more might have gone to their rescue, but it would have meant that those who were in the water would have swarmed aboard and sunk her.

15 April 1912

Memories of Waterloo

Edmund Wheatley

...About ten o'clock, the order came to clean out the muskets and fresh load them. Half an allowance of rum was then issued, and we descended into the plain, and took our positions in solid Squares. When this was arranged as per order, we were ordered to remain in our position but, if we like, to lay down, which the battalion did [as well as] the officers in the rere.

I took this opportunity of surveying our situation. It was singular to perceive the shoals of Cavalry and artillery suddenly in our rere all arranged in excellent order as if by a magic wand. The whole of the Horse Guards stood behind us. For my part I thought they were at Knightsbridge barracks or prancing on St James' Street.

A Ball whizzed in the air. Up we started simultaneously. I looked at my watch. It was just eleven o'clock, Sunday (Eliza just in Church at Wallingford or at Abingdon) morning. In five minutes a stunning noise took place and a shocking havock commenced.

One could almost feel the undulation of the air from the multitude of cannon shot. The first man who fell was five files on my left. With the utmost distortion of feature he lay on his side and shrivelling up every muscle of the body he twirled his elbow round and round in acute agony, then dropped lifeless, dying as it's called a death of glory, heaving his last breath on the field of fame. *Dieu m'engarde!*

A black consolidated body was soon seen approaching and we distinguished by sudden flashes of light from the sun's rays, the iron-cased cavalry of the enemy. Shouts of 'Stand firm!' 'Stand fast!' were heard from the little squares around and very quickly these gigantic fellows were upon us.

No words can convey the sensation we felt on seeing these heavy-armed bodies advancing at full gallop against us, flourishing their sabres in the air, striking their armour with the handles, the sun gleaming on the steel. The long horse hair, dishevelled by the wind, bore an appearance confounding the senses to an astonishing disorder. But we dashed them back as cooly as the sturdy rock repels the ocean's foam. The sharp-toothed bayonet bit many an adventurous fool, and on all sides we presented our bristly points like the peevish porcupines assailed by clamorous dogs.

The Horse Guards then came up and drove them back; and although the sight is shocking 'tis beautiful to see the skirmish of Cavalry.

The French made repeated attacks of this kind. But we stood firm as the ground we stood on, and two long hours were employed in these successive attacks.

About two o'clock the Cavalry ceased annoying and the warfare took a new turn. In order to destroy our squares, the enemy filled the air with shells, howitzers and bombs, so that every five or six minutes, the whole Battalion lay on its face then sprang up again when [the danger] was over.

The Prince of Orange gallop'd by, screaming out like a new born infant, 'Form into line! Form into line!' And we obeyed.

About this time the battle grew faint and a mutual cannonade with musketry amused us for one and a half hours, during which time I walked up and down chatting and joking with the young officers who had not [until] then smelt powder.

An ammunition cart blew up near us, smashing men and horses. I took a calm survey of the field around and felt shocked at the sight of broken armour, lifeless bodies, murdered horses, shattered wheels, caps, helmets, swords, muskets, pistols, still and silent. Here and there a frightened horse would rush across the plain trampling on the dying and the dead. Three or four poor wounded animals standing on three legs, the other dangling before [them]. We killed several of these unfortunate beasts and it would have been an equal Charity to have perform'd the same operation on the wriggling, feverish, mortally lacerated soldiers as they rolled on the ground.

About four o'clock the battle was renewed with uncommon ardour. We still stood in line. The carnage was frightful. The balls which missed us mowed down the Dutch behind us, and swept away many of the closely embattled Cavalry behind them.

I saw a cannon ball take away a Colonel of the Nassau Regiment so cleanly that the horse never moved from under him. While [I was] busy in keeping the men firm in their ranks, closing up the vacuities as the balls swept off the men, inspecting the fallen to detect deception [or] subterfuge, a regiment of Cuirassiers darted like a thunderbolt among us. At the instant a squadron of Horse Guards dashed up to our rescue. In the confusion of the moment I made [for] the Colours to defend them. And we succeeded with infinite difficulty in rallying the men again.

I parried with great good fortune a back stroke from a horseman as he flew by me and Captain Sander had a deep slice from the same fellow on the head the instant after.

The battalion once more formed into a solid square, in which we remained the [whole] afternoon.

I felt the ardor of the fight increase very much within me, from the uncommon fury of the engagement.

Just then I fired a slain soldier's musket until my shoulder was nearly jellied and my mouth was begrimed with gunpowder to such a degree that I champed the gritty composition unknowingly.

Nothing could equal the splendour and terror of the scene. Charge after charge succeeded in constant succession. The clashing of swords, the clattering of musketry, the hissing of balls, and shouts and clamours produced a sound, jarring and confounding the senses, as if hell and the Devil were in evil contention.

About this time I saw the Duke of Wellington running from a charge of Cavalry towards the Horse Guards, waving his hat to beckon them to encounter.

All our artillery in front fell into the French power, the bombardiers skulking under the carriages. But five minutes put them again into our hands and the men creeping out applied the match and sent confusion and dismay into the retreating enemy.

Several times were these charges renewed and as often defeated. Charge met charge and all was pellmell. The rays of the sun glittered on the clashing swords as the two opposing bodies closed in fearful combat and our musket balls clattered on the shining breastplates like a hail shower.

As I stood in the square I looked down, I recollect, to take a pinch of snuff and thought of the old ballad, which I had seen somewhere, of the aged Nurse who describes the glorious battles of Marlborough to the child. After each relation of valour and victory, the infant [says]

'Ten thousand slain you say and more?
What did they kill each other for?'
'Indeed I cannot tell,' said she,
'But 'twas a famous victory.'*

The field was now thickened with heaps of bodies and shattered instruments. Carcases of men and beasts lay promiscuously entwined. Aide-de-Camps scoured across with inconceivable velocity. All was hurry and indefatigable exertion. The small squares on our right kept up incessant firings and the fight was as obstinate as at the commencement.

The Duke of Wellington passed us twice, slowly and cooly.

No advantage as yet was discernible on either side. The French Cavalry were less annoying. Their brave, repeated assaults had cost them very dear.

About six o'clock a passe-parole ran down the line – not to be disheartened, as the Prussians were coming up to our left, which news we received with loud cheers. And on looking [to] the left I perceived at some distance a dark swarm moving out of a thick wood. In twenty minutes a fresh cannonading began as if in rere of the French and the battle raged with increased vehemence.

A French Regiment of Infantry before us opposite the Farm house called the holy hedge (La Haye Sainte) advanced considerably just then and poured a destructive fire into our Battalion.

* The diarist is faultily recollecting *The Battle of Blenheim* by Robert Southey

Colonel Ompteda ordered us instantly into line to charge, with a strong injunction to 'walk' forward, until he gave the word. When within sixty yards he cried 'Charge', we ran forward huzzaing. The trumpet sounded and no one but a soldier can describe the thrill one instantly feels in such an awful moment. At the bugle sound the French stood until we reached them. I ran by Colonel Ompteda who cried out, 'That's right, Wheatley!'

I found myself in contact with a French officer but ere we could decide, he fell by an unknown hand. I then ran at a drummer, but he leaped over a ditch through a hedge in which he stuck fast. I heard a cry of, 'The Cavalry! The Cavalry!' But so eager was I that I did not mind it at the moment, and when on the eve of dragging the Frenchman back (his iron-bound hat having saved him from a Cut) I recollect no more. On recovering my senses, I look'd up and found myself, bareheaded, in a clay ditch with a violent headache. Close by me lay Colonel Ompteda on his back, his head stretched back with his mouth open, and a hole in his throat. A Frenchman's arm across my leg.

So confused was I that I did not remember I was on the field of Battle at the moment. Lifting up a little, I look'd over the edge of the ditch and saw the backs of a French Regiment and all the day's employment instantly suggested itself to my mind. Suddenly I distinguished some voices and heard one say '*En voici! En voici!*'

I lay down as dead, retaining my breath, and fancied I was shot in the back of my head. Presently a fellow cries, '*Voici un autre b.*' And a tug at my epaulette bespoke his commission. A thought struck me – he would turn me round to rifle my pockets. So starting up, I leaped up the ditch; but a swimming seized me and I was half on the ground when the fellow thrust his hand in my collar, grinning, '*Ou va's tu, chein?*' I begged him to let me pick up my cap and he dragged me into the house...

June 1815

They May Be Watching You

Marion Dewhirst

Have you ever been for the day to the seaside, or strolled on Hampstead Heath, or merely talked to a friend in a bus or tram, and suddenly realized that someone was recording your conversation in a little note book?

The chances are that the scribe was neither a plain-clothes detective, nor a lunatic, but merely a Mass-Observer. The chances are, also, that – if you hadn't a guilty conscience, in which case, doubtless, you melted unobtrusively away, fearing the worst – you turned on the recording angel, and said indignantly: 'Here, what do you mean by eavesdropping like that? You ought to be ashamed of yourself,' or words to that effect.

How We Behave

Then, again, the chances are that you have been Mass-Observed and *don't know it* . . .

Mass Observation sets out to be a new science; or, rather, a new method of finding out scientific truths.

The originators of it reasoned that if a body of information were available as to **why we do and say certain things, how we behave in special sets of circumstances, this would help us to know ourselves and other people better.**

So they issued an appeal for helpers – people who would be willing to keep their eyes and ears open, and write down exactly what they saw or heard.

The first big thing they attempted was a survey of Coronation Day. Every Mass-Observer wrote down everything that happened to him or her on that day, down to the smallest detail. The published results made a most interesting record of just what the popular reaction is to this sort of ceremony.

Another survey – recorded in the recently published report of the first year's work in Mass-Observation (Lindsay Drummond. 3s. 6d.) – dealt with not one particular day, but a particular habit – cigarette smoking.

Tappers or Non-Tappers

It was found that about 17 per cent. of smokers feel definite hostility to non-smokers, because a non-smoker does not seem 'one of them'; that 44 per cent. of men and 64 per cent. of women smokers began to smoke purely because other people do.

Various smokers' habits were recorded. 54 per cent. of smokers tap their cigarette before placing it in their mouths, 52 per cent. of 'tappers' place the tapped end in their mouths, and 21 per cent. the untapped end – but hardly any of them can give a reason for their tapping!

At present the Mass-Observers are working on a Northern industrial town – Bolton. Public houses, football pools, the newspapers people read, the things they laugh at – all the details making up everyday life are being examined and tabulated.

Its Use?

The use of it all? The machinery for an analysis of motives, feelings and behaviour, may become of inestimable service to us, living as we do in an age when, while the mechanical sciences have advanced tremendously, the social sciences have lagged far behind.

18 June 1938

War Begins at Home

A National Panel Diarist

3 September 1939

A momentous day. 11–11.15 am. The Prime Minister is about to break the news of the war. It is inevitable, I have been convinced of it since last September. Hope against hope for peace, impossible with the greed and evilness of humanity spreading.

War, – how ghastly, we must live a day at a time and never think of all the plans for the coming months.

I am glad I have nearly finished bagging the front of our shelter, it will be as near gas and splinter proof as it is possible to make it. I have a great admiration for Poland, during this conflict I hope England regains the prestige it has lost.

The evacuation has gone off smoothly, this part, although fairly dangerous, has not gone.

Have decided to keep Jacqueline with me, no one else would bother with her special diet.

Sept. 4

News of the *Athenia* [torpedoed by a German submarine] has just come through, I hope to God the world leaves Britain and France and Poland to wipe Germany from the face of the earth, until we do we shall never have any peace.

Fancy Jacqueline deciding to run a temperature, can I take her down in the shelter should an air raid come or do I have to stay in the house?

I have done one bag too many for the shelter I have strained my side a bit, it never rains but what it pours, the tank has decided to leak and father says (worried like), 'If you have been working too hard it is a sign of hysteria.' My retort was, 'I didn't know one had to have hysteria in one's foot to cause it to slip on a slippery clay.'

10.30 p.m. Have gone to bed hoping there will not be an air raid tonight, I'm too tired to care anyway.

Sept. 5

The world around me has settled down, the women don't stand around quite so long gossiping. I see the same faces going to work every morning at exactly the same time, the only difference is, now they all carry gas masks.

The windows every night become a little darker. The children play in the streets exactly the same. They still pop to the Hucksters for '½ of flour and 2d of corned beef!'

The shopkeeper told me that that class of people do not shop a day at a time but a meal at a time, they had no stock in [...] That class of people will muddle through the war the same as they muddle through in peace time, the one shining light will be that the sons that go to war will find themselves in time and so save themselves their parents' existence. I heard that at the Co-op shop they had sold three weeks' sugar supply on the Thursday and Friday before the war was declared.

Sept. 6

I am running a temperature now, I have been working too hard and caught a chill, the only interest I show in the war tonight is to hope to goodness there isn't a raid because I couldn't go down to the shelter if there was. My husband, generally most reserved, has done more talking this past fortnight than I've ever known him do in his life.

I am very conscientious, it annoys me when I talk to people asking them if they fill the bath every night, have they a case ready with every thing in ready to dash to safety, the different answers, 'I trust in the Lord,' I said, 'If you haven't prepared the Lord can't save you from gas nor any thing else.' Another says, 'I don't really think anything will happen do you, its a long way from Germany.' Next door is a young baby four months, they haven't had a shelter, it would mean spoiling the garden, 'The Lord will look after the baby.' Next door the other side they haven't one, too much trouble, what do I do, that's my problem? offer mine?

September 1939

London Burning

A Canadian Sergeant

I had been taking supper with my sister, who is an ambulance driver, and at about half-past twelve I stepped outside to have a look round, in the hope that I'd be lucky enough to see one of our night fighters score a victory – and I was quite surprised to see fires of considerable size blazing about two miles away. I slipped a coat on and walked to the top of a hill, the better to see – and the higher I got, the more serious it looked. From where I stood, I could look over the Regents Park area to Baker Street Tube Station, and beyond to Marble Arch, Piccadilly, Hyde Park, and the West End in general.

It was a holocaust of flames and smoke; bursting bombs, and more and more incendiaries starting more fires. Broken gas mains were flaming, and there was a veritable devil's tattoo of anti-aircraft fire and machine guns. It's awful to think that such a destructive and inhumane thing as an air raid, in which people are dying and homes being blasted, *could* be beautiful – but actually from a distance it was a sight worth seeing.

From my eminence, it was as though I was looking into a vast cauldron, from which arose a dull red glow, shot through with terrific, vivid white flashes; while clouds of smoke, dust and sparks billowed up and caused the moon to change from pale green to a rich orange tinge. On my left was a battery of three light guns, whose muzzle-blast reminded you of the yapping of a bad-tempered terrier dog. Dead ahead, another battery of heavier guns were going off with a report like a giant firecracker exploding in an iron drainpipe. Then there was a crash of the heavy-calibre guns that might easily be mistaken for an exploding enemy bomb. Firing in groups of three, combined with all the other sounds you hear in an air raid, it is like a sort of symphony orchestra.

Through all the noise and confusion, there is a constant consciousness of whistles; as an inevitable background to any air raid, there are always police whistles, wardens' whistles, signals from rescue parties, and other whistles that impress themselves on your mind by their constancy. They never seem loud or close at hand – yet you *always* hear them. One of my clearest rememberances of air raids will always be of this particular sound.

Well, anyway, I stood watching the great fire, and said to myself, 'I'll walk down to the next corner, to see if I can see it better from there.' When I got there, the *next* corner looked a better vantage point – and so on, until I was rushing up the street towards the area that had been paid particular attention by the *Luftwaffe*. On the way down, I stopped to talk to a group of fire-watchers, and we all suddenly heard the oddest sound – like the sound of old brass cowbells at home, that go *clunk-clunk*, instead of ringing clearly. The sound was overhead and all around us, coming nearer. It was such a gentle sound that no one took alarm, and we finally started to hear things falling in the road. A policeman came up, and told us they were probably booby trap bombs – that is, a tin of fifty De Reszke cigarettes – which explode when any attempt is made to open them! Several had been found already. We spent a fruitless ten minutes trying to locate them, and then I continued on down to the fire.

Just as I was leaving the group, a big one started to come down, and it sounded as if it was landing fairly close – so the five special wardens flung themselves down on the ground like so many rag dolls! But when it did land, it didn't explode. I continued on down the street, past Lord's Cricket Ground, and rounding the curve, came in full sight of the fire. It was ghastly, yet magnificent. At the extremity of the street a broken gas main was flaming like fury. Flames towered up 50 feet or so and brought into sharp relief the tiny scurrying figures of the Auxiliary Fire Service and the other workers, as they raced between the flames and me.

I hurried down, and the first job presented itself in the person of a girl, who asked me to help put out incendiaries that she had noticed in a row of flats round the corner. Several of us polished them off, and in the doing of it, I got drenched. I was flinging a pail of water at a blazing hole in the ceiling, just when a guy on the floor above was flinging a pail of water at a blazing hole in the floor – the consequences were staggering, as the pailful caught me squarely in the chest! All this time, *that man* was circling about overhead, dropping things on the fire. Strangely enough, you don't hear them explode if you're working hard – or else, it may be that you don't care!

Further down the street I saw a fireman struggling to get a hose into a four-storey building, the top floor of which was well alight; so an Air Force bloke and myself gave him a hand, and up to the top we went, by a circular stairway. On reaching the top, the fireman said, 'Hold on to the hose, while I go down and start the pumper.' We were holding on like mad – but nothing happened. So the other chap, fearing that something had happened to the fireman, went to the window to have a look – and at that moment the water came on! The hose started leaping and bucking like mad, and as the first surge of water came spurting through, it bashed me up against the wall, as if I were a straw. We soon had it under control, though, and as three men trying to point a hose seemed to me one too many, I went down to the street, to see if I could help elsewhere.

All I can rememer of the next two hours is being on a roof, and my foot going through the slates and cutting my shin; climbing endless stairs with sand and water; kicking down locked doorways to gain access to houses on fire, and holding the hose. The house whose roof I stuck my foot through we couldn't save – and yet the lady who owned it had the pluck to crack jokes and make us tea, while her top storey was blazing.

Next I spotted a rescue party hacking at the indescribable wreckage of a house – mattresses, birdcages, tables, linoleum, bedding, chesterfields, lumber, steel, bricks and dust, all welded into a seemingly immovable mass. 'There's three in that lot!' said a grim-looking old cuss – so off with the coat, and everybody tore into the pile, and miracle of miracles, we found the man of the house alive – shaken but unhurt – lying in a small groove-like space, sheltered by flooring boards from above. He was able to tell us exactly where to find his wife and mother, and although we could see them and hand them water, it was another hour and a half before we got them out – both almost completely unhurt.

By now almost every other roof for blocks around was blazing. Not just *small* fires – but one which everybody at home would turn out to see, if they occurred in London, Ontario. There were 20 fires to every fireman, and being old-fashioned buildings, with steep pitched roofs, thousands of gables and chimney-pots, it was very difficult to get at them. The houses all butted together, so that if one fire got out of control, it pretty well spelt *finis* to the others in that block. There were many unusual silhouettes, as churches and other buildings of unusual design would be a seething mass of flames inside, and the lovely arches, and odd corners with their gargoyles, etc. would stand out framed blackly against the angry red of the inner fire.

At last it began to get light, and the last of the Hun raiders dropped his load and scooted. The anti-aircraft bursts pursuing him grew farther and farther away. I felt about done in, so I trudged home, tired but happy – glad to have been some help in London's biggest Blitz so far.

May 1941

The House Fell About Our Ears!

A Nottingham Mother

Ours was a terrible experience. Fortunately we had moved the beds downstairs the night before the raid, as Jerry had been around all week. On this night the sirens went at nine o'clock, while we were listening to the news – but we didn't take much notice, as usually nothing happens. I was making some blackout curtains from material I had bought that day, and my husband went upstairs to the small back bedroom to watch the searchlights. About 20 minutes later we heard a Jerry circling round – but we still didn't bother.

Then all of a sudden there were four terrific bangs, and I flew in and picked up baby and dashed into the pantry – which I thought was the safest place. But to my horror I saw flames spurting up outside the window. I called to my husband that there were incendiary bombs outside, and when he went out, the whole place was alight; there was one in every garden down our road, and the men around were busy putting them out. We thought the plane had gone for good, when suddenly we heard him coming back. I dived under the dining-room table; G. was standing by the door; when suddenly there was a terrible explosion that rocked the house. The next explosion put out the light; the third struck the house, and it all came down on top of us.

The smell from the bomb was *terrible* – I thought we had been gassed. My next thought was that we should have to wait until we were dug out. I could feel the debris on my back – but just then my husband managed to reach me, and we tried to scramble out. I had put the baby right underneath me for protection; when it all fell, she just let out one awful scream, and was so quiet after that, I thought she *must* be hurt or something. But she was alright. G. and I, with the baby, ran along the road to a house we know that has a basement; there we sheltered until the all-clear sounded at four o'clock. What a night! The planes were going over every few minutes, and all of us in that basement crouched over our babies, in case anything else fell.

Morning came, and we were able to see the damage. All the upstairs of our house was gone, and the front of the house was nowhere to be seen. The room we were in was the only room at all recognizable. Other houses near ours were either completely demolished, or else had their backs blown in, and all had their doors and windows blown out. At five o'clock in the morning, the wardens took everybody round to the church schoolroom for hot tea, and kept us there, as they suspected there were delayed action bombs about. Nearly all our stuff has gone – a lot we can never replace – but we have our lives, *and* the baby, and that is far more important.

1941

Visiting Hiroshima

Marcel Junod

The bare cone of Fujiyama was just visible on the horizon as we flew over the 'inland sea' which lay beneath us like a lavender-blue carpet picked out in green and yellow with its numerous promontories and wooded islands...

...Towards midday a huge white patch appeared on the ground below us. This chalky desert, looking almost like ivory in the sun, surrounded by a crumble of twisted ironwork and ash heaps, was all that remained of Hiroshima...

...The journalist described the main official buildings of the town, which were built of reinforced concrete and dominated a sea of low-roofed Japanese houses extending over six miles to the wooded hills I could see in the distance.

'The town was not much damaged,' he explained. 'It had suffered very little from the bombing. There were only two minor raids, one on March 19 last by a squadron of American naval planes, and one on April 30 by a Flying Fortress.

'On August 6 there wasn't a cloud in the sky above Hiroshima, and a mild, hardly perceptible wind blew from the south. Visibility was almost perfect for ten or twelve miles.

'At nine minutes past seven in the morning an air raid warning sounded and four American B-29 planes appeared. To the north of the town two of them turned and made off to the south and disappeared in the direction of the Shoho Sea. The other two, after having circled the neighbourhood of Shukai, flew off at high speed southwards in the direction of the Bingo Sea.

'At 7.31 the all-clear was given. Feeling themselves in safety people came out of their shelters and went about their affairs and the work of the day began.

'Suddenly a glaring whitish pinkish light appeared in the sky accompanied by an unnatural tremor which was followed almost immediately by a wave of suffocating heat and a wind which swept away everything in its path.

'Within a few seconds the thousands of people in the streets and the gardens in the centre of the town were scorched by a wave of searing heat. Many were killed instantly, others lay writhing on the ground screaming in agony from the intolerable pain of their burns. Everything standing upright in the way of the blast, walls, houses, factories and other buildings, was annihilated and the debris spun round in a whirlwind and was carried up into the air. Trams were picked up and tossed aside as though they had neither weight nor solidity. Trains were flung off the rails as though they were toys. Horses, dogs and cattle suffered the same fate as human beings. Every living thing was petrified in an attitude of indescribable suffering. Even the vegetation did not escape. Trees went up in flames, the rice plants lost their greenness, the grass burned on the ground like dry straw.

'Beyond the zone of utter death in which nothing remained alive houses collapsed in a whirl of beams, bricks and girders. Up to about three miles from the centre of the explosion lightly built houses were flattened as though they had been built of cardboard. Those who were inside were either killed or wounded. Those who managed to extricate themselves by some miracle found themselves surrounded by a ring of fire. And the few who succeeded in making their way to safety generally died 20 or 30 days later from the delayed effects of the deadly gamma rays. Some of the reinforced concrete or stone buildings remained standing but their interiors were completely gutted by the blast.

'About half an hour after the explosion whilst the sky all around Hiroshima was still cloudless a fine rain began to fall on the town and went on for about five minutes. It was caused by the sudden rise of overheated air to a great height, where it condensed and fell back as rain. Then a violent wind rose and the fires extended with terrible rapidity, because most Japanese houses are built only of timber and straw.

'By evening the fire began to die down and then it went out. There was nothing left to burn. Hiroshima had ceased to exist.'

The Japanese broke off and then pronounced one word with indescribable but restrained emotion: 'Look.'

We were then rather less than four miles away from the Aioi Bridge, which was immediately beneath the explosion, but already the roofs of the houses around us had lost their tiles and the grass was yellow along the roadside. At three miles from the centre of the devastation the houses were already destroyed, their roofs had fallen in and the beams jutted out from the wreckage of their walls. But so far it was only the usual spectacle presented by towns damaged by ordinary high explosives.

About two and a half miles from the centre of the town all the buildings had been burnt out and destroyed. Only traces of the foundations and piles of debris and rusty charred ironwork were left. This zone was like the devastated areas of Tokyo, Osaka and Kobé after the mass fall of incendiaries.

At three-quarters of a mile from the centre of the explosion nothing at all was left. Everything had disappeared. It was stony waste littered with debris and twisted girders. The incandescent breath of the fire had swept away every obstacle and all that remained upright were one or two fragments of stone walls and a few stoves which had remained incongruously on their base.

We got out of the car and made our way slowly through the ruins into the centre of the dead city. Absolute silence reigned in the whole necropolis.

9 September 1945

Give me Copy, Fast

John Diamond

As part of an annual competition run by *The Guardian* John Diamond offers advice to the would-be feature writer.

...There are some dozen books in print and half a dozen correspondence courses on writing for the freelance market. Most large local education authorities run an evening class on the subject, and there are any number of short courses and weekend seminars which, at a couple of hundred quid a throw, promise to turn you into a writer.

None of them can. All most can promise is the chance of the odd low-paid piece in a hobby or specialist magazines and the chance to see your name in print. If you don't know that a newspaper feature should have an opening paragraph which compels the reader to make it to the second par, that you rarely need an exclamation mark, that the last paragraph is as important as the first, then I have nothing to offer you.

What I can tell you is what an editor expects from a freelance apart from good writing...

- **Your copy should look professional.**

Given the average editor's tendency to bin anything that's too obviously the work of an amateur it's as well to look as if you know what you're doing.

Whatever the Clackheaton Postal School of Journalism would have you believe, I have never seen a commissioned newspaper m/s which carries its own cover sheet bearing nothing but a title and a copyright notice. Sub-editors write titles, or, rather, headlines, feature writers don't.

Type – never, ever, write – the copy, with widish margins, double spaced on one side of paper. The top line of each sheet should contain your name (and usually just your surname), the name of the editor to whose attention the copy should be directed and the section of the paper – features, media, whatever – they look after, a single catchword which is likely to be unique to that story, and the numbers of the page. At the bottom of each sheet type 'MORE' and at the bottom of the last page 'ENDS'.

Many of these rules are based on newspaper practice before computerization, but no matter: this is still what copy is meant to look like.

- **Decide precisely what it is you're writing about.**

Newspapers aren't hot on stream of consciousness writing, writing that strays too far off the subject, writing which runs out of steam halfway through. There are many full-time writers who won't be able to remember the last time they wrote down a list of points to make, quotes they need or the order in which they will bind the whole together. But if the last piece you wrote was your English homework, make the sort of preliminary notes your teacher recommended.

- **Keep to length.**

It's easy to ramble on for 5,000 words on almost any subject: keeping to a tightly written 1,500 or 800 words takes discipline and skill. If you are writing on spec then look carefully at the paper you're writing for. If its features run to 1,500 words then that's what you need to write. The occasional 5,000 worder by some household name is a dispensation granted by the editor only to household names.

- **You're not there to write about yourself.**

The sort of gonzo journalism where you indulge yourself in noting nothing more than your responses to your subject is fit only for fifth form magazines and the collected works of Hunter S. Thompson. If you are interviewing somebody the idea is to get their words into the paper, not yours. If you are writing about an event or some social phenomenon then let the participants describe it.

Having said that, it's part of the job to put those words into context, to suggest why the interviewee is saying them, to suggest in which way the words are being said. You should bring sounds, colours, smells, feelings to the piece but the words you use should help the reader understand what the event or the person was like rather than help them understand how clever you are with words.

- **Be accurate.**

It's tempting to quote what you'd like somebody to say, or what you think they meant to say. Don't. Write what they do say. Unless a subject's inarticulacy is germane to the piece there's no need to draw attention to it and there's nothing wrong with tidying up a quote for public consumption. Quote vernacularisms by all means, but try not to write in dialect or local accent: it gets tedious after a very short while.

Many feature writers use a tape recorder, in part because interviewees tend to find a note book too permanent a reminder that what they're saying is being taken down and might be used against them. A recorder is also useful for taking notes to yourself and very useful to play to a jury when a litigious subject denies what you reported.

I find it's worth establishing ground rules before you start taping. I tell any subject not used to speaking to a journalist that 'off the record' means precisely that, that anything labelled 'non-attributable' won't be attributed and that they can ask me to turn off the tape.

- **Kill your babies.**

Go through the copy cutting out any good gag that doesn't add to the piece, any opinion that isn't relevant, any padding put in while you were thinking of what to write next.

Now here's your assignment. Saturday Night with... It's as wide a brief as you could imagine, but it's up to you to narrow it down. You have been commissioned by an editor to write 1,500 words (100 each way is allowable, but no more) on a Saturday night in a place, with a person or at an event. You choose which.

It shouldn't, for preference, be somewhere that all readers will have experienced: a very few writers might get a piece out of something as mundane as Saturday Night At The Milton Keynes Multiplex Cinema but many more would stand a chance of making a story out of the last Saturday night before their local fleapit closes down.

You'd have to be an extremely good writer to get 1,500 words out of Saturday Night Hanging Out At The Arndale Centre, but there might just possibly be a piece in spending all Saturday night talking to the people drifting through a 24-hour supermarket. Saturday night with a local police crew or in a casualty ward might be interesting if unoriginal. Saturday night with any person or group for whom Saturday, or a particular Saturday, is special is worth thinking about especially if it's a local story that is a metaphor for something happening nationally.

Whatever. You fill in the miss ing words and write the piece. The judges will be looking for good, sharp writing, appropriate quotations and background research, and solid evidence of your ability to make us feel that we were there. We won't be looking for political manifestos, creative writing coursework, poems or fiction. The competition is about journalism...

17 August 1992

Newspaper History

John Frost

It had been an uneventful shift. The time was now 2 am on Sunday 5 October 1930.

Journalists on the *Sunday Express* were getting ready to pack it in for the night, when news came over the wire – 45 people burned to death on the maiden voyage of the largest thing ever to fly, the R101 airship. It had crashed into a hillside in northern France.

The *Sunday Express* had a scoop. 'Late Stop' on the paper decided to put through an edition, recalling writers and printers who had already gone to bed. Within three hours of the crash a special edition was on the streets. The news was being read throughout Britain while the embers were still cooling in France.

My first memory of newspaper collecting was of going out on that Sunday to buy a copy of *The News of the World* which also produced a 'special' edition.

There isn't a scoop like the story of R101 every day. There are relatively few, in fact, in the 25,000 newspapers I have collected subsequently, but every day, in virtually every country in the world, newspapers are on sale with some dramatic story hours, minutes even after the event. Aided extensively now by the same technology that brings television and wireless to people instantaneously.

Newspapers are essentially the same as they have been for a century-and-a-half. They still, and will always have to, rely on machinery to produce a concrete end-product, and after all the rush to get the product on sale, they are discarded quicker than almost any other commodity.

The importance of the newspaper lies in this urgency and immediacy. Through its pages arrives the first opportunity to take in information, reflect and then form an opinion of what has been read. Without pretending that newspapers always provide the right facts, or the right interpretation of events as they happen, they do provide something which is much more important, a chronicle of history *as it is being made*. The story, as written in the newspaper of the day is, for most people, the reality of the situation. A slick headline becomes someone else's opinion. 'It was in the papers. It must be true.'

Looking back at yesterday's papers gives an insight into how the public received the news at the time. This, to me, is at the heart of the reasons why newspapers are so stimulating.

As an example of this, papers reporting the outbreak of the Second World War are particularly evocative. There is no way of getting closer to the experience, or bringing it back vividly to mind than picking up a newspaper with the front page news: 'FIRST DAY OF THE SECOND GREAT WAR... "We fight against evil things – brute force, bad faith, injustice, oppression and persecution – and against them I am certain that the right will prevail," the Premier said.'

Balanced against such reports of the important moments in history, there are times when 'stories' which have covered a front page are later proved to be the result of a false lead, or are just plainly inaccurate. On 1 February 1970 *The People* banner headline read: HORROR IN A NAMELESS VILLAGE – BRITISH GUILT REVEALED. The story unveiled a massacre of 25 suspected terrorists by British troops in Malaya in 1948, and caused a political stir at the time. Exactly six months later this seven-line 'filler' appeared in the *Daily Mail*: 'A Scotland Yard investigator has found that charges in a Sunday newspaper that members of a patrol of Scots Guards massacred 25 suspected terrorists in the Malay jungle in 1948 were unfounded.'

The importance of this example is not that the incident did or did not take place. It was a controversy created by a newspaper; a piece of history that will not be found in history books, only the papers of the time.

Occasionally, newspapers help to make history. The Spanish-American War of 1898 was dubbed the 'Newspapers' War' because of its exploitation by American newspaper proprietors to boost circulations. Randolph Hearst, the legendary press king, owner at the time of the *San Francisco Examiner* and the *New York Journal*, decided that the American people wanted war with Spain over Cuba, and he wanted more readers for his papers. When one of his artists asked to be recalled from Cuba because of the lack of activity, Hearst cabled: 'Please remain. You furnish the pictures and I'll furnish the war.' The war happened. In the year before World War II, Lord Beaverbrook's *Daily Express* proclaimed: NO WAR, THIS YEAR OR NEXT. His attempt at influencing the course of events was rather less effective than Hearst's, but the efforts both resulted in coloured, but colourful, journalism.

Where newspapers come into their own, I believe, is on the occasions when they report events which subsequently do get into the history books. They provide *real* colour through their style, language, pictures, of what it was like to be there...

1984

The Tragedy of the *Titanic*

A great wrong has been committed in the world. Safety can never be absolute. But we are not dealing with the inevitable in this case. We are dealing with a preventable disaster, for which no man upon the *Titanic* was mainly to blame. By error and inadequacy on shore, by unimaginative routine and official inertia, by the decay of national interest in mercantile seamanship sixteen hundred souls have been sacrificed. She had been warned that ice was thicker in the path than usual. Well, vigilance at look-out and on the bridge would perceive it. At evening the *Titanic* – following, remember, the route of possible death deliberately chosen by the shipping companies in concert as against the slightly longer path of assured safety to the south – was in the region which can only be called the great ship-trap of the seas. The companies have ordered in the last few days that the route shall be changed. Why did they not change it before? Why was the *Titanic* sent into the ship-trap when it is certain that by making the course only a few hours longer the sixteen hundred lives now sacrificed would never have been lost?

There are other issues not less urgent. It would surpass the sombre power of a Dantesque imagination to enforce the horror of this commonplace of ocean traffic: that the modern ocean liner with two or three thousand souls on board only provides enough boat accommodation for about a third of her passengers and crew. There is no technical reason why the proportion should not be largely increased or why other devices should not be employed, giving every man a chance for life.

Behind the grief for the *Titanic* is a sense of bitter waste. There will be a cloud upon the conscience of England and America until the lessons of the saddest tragedy wrought amidst the peaceful nations in the whole history of the seas, shall be so applied that the lives of those who did well upon the *Titanic* shall not have been offered in vain.

The Observer, 21 April 1912

The New World: True Freedom or a 'Peace of Terror'

New York, Saturday. The second world war is ending. It has lasted six years for Britain, four for Russia, and three and a half for the United States. It has lasted 14 years for China. Mankind threw into this war all that it possessed and drew upon its descendants as well. Its dead are as yet uncalculable. Certainly, civilians contributed as many and probably far more casualties than armies, and this is not over. Those who perished in the cities of Hiroshima and Nagasaki died, we are told, 'a death no one ever died before.'

At the outbreak there were the following 'Great Powers' on earth – the British Empire, the United States, Germany, Japan, Italy, France, and the Soviet Union. Britain was the strongest naval Power; Germany the strongest land and air Power; Japan the leading Power of Asia; France was rated high; the Soviet Union was rated low. The United States was rated strongest economically and technologically, dubious militarily, inactive politically.

Today the United States is the strongest Power on the sea and in the air, and, with economic and technical factors added, overwhelmingly strongest from any point of view. Great Britain has lost the mastery of the seas, and the Soviet Union, which has no challenger on the European continent, is checked only by American technology.

Until the invention of the atomic bomb, there was some chance of stabilization on that basis. But with the perspective that rival continents can blow up each other and the planet, this hope is no longer tenable. The two great complexes of power left from this war, Anglo-American and Soviet, cannot go to war against each other. And no one else can even dream of going to war against them.

The message of the Unknown Soldier comes in the very words of Christ, 'Ye must be born again – or we have died in vain.' He needs no wreath and wants no tomb, he, who carried into this war so vast a burden of doubt, so great a light of hope, the doubts and the hopes of the whole of suffering mankind.

The Observer, 12 August 1945

Unreasonable Behaviour

Don McCullin

...In those days there was a firmly set out path for a young man to follow. First he got the violence out of his system, then he went out with a girl for a two-year period before he married her and settled down. To my surprise, Christine's parents accepted me as her regular chap, deceived perhaps by the wholesome effects of my mother's garden hose. Yet, despite her civilizing influence, I had not reached the end of my wild youth. I went for a bloke one day who started pestering us at a bus stop and at the end of the fight fox-trotted with Christine and a broken lip round Hornsey Town Hall. But the most bizarre fight was my last in Finsbury Park.

We were on our way home from the funeral of a girl who had committed suicide over one of the local boys, and were in an emotional state, when one of the hard nuts in the back of my old Ford Consul demanded a pee in the Holloway Road. In his haste to run off up an alleyway, he broke the wing mirror. I got out of the car and called a name after him. I should have gone for him while he was peeing for that is when it is most difficult to carry on a fight, but I was not fighting mad, only annoyed. The next thing I knew was him standing before me, flourishing a brick in front of my face. I managed to hit him in the ribs, and then I grabbed the brick and hit him across the head with it. I kept on hitting him as the blood oozed from his head. I felt it was either him or me.

Then I said, 'Have you had enough now?' His reply was to smash his head into my face. As we stood there, both pouring blood, he said calmly, 'I think that's about even.'

We got back in the car, and I drove him to the Royal Northern Hospital to get his head stitched up. I didn't know him well but he always had a friendly greeting for me after that. Christine was unnerved by this sort of violence, but she remained loyal to me. Arriving home at Fonthill Road from one of our regular dates at the cinema, we found my mother, unusually, still up. She had news.

'That gang you hang around with at Gray's,' she said, 'they're in trouble. A policeman's been killed up there.'

It turned out that a man older than was usual in the gangs had been at the centre of the barney. Ronald Marwood, a 25-year-old scaffolder from Islington, had gone to the Academy with a knife to settle some vengeful argument, though knuckle-dusters were as far as things went usually. He had probably thought only of intimidation, but when the gangs took sides and fought on the pavement outside, a policeman had tried to wedge himself between the opposing sides and had been stabbed in the back. He died from loss of blood. Marwood fled, but his father persuaded him to give himself up.

Those of us who lived in Finsbury Park spoke of little else but the killing in the next few weeks. It also focused national thinking on the growing phenomenon of delinquent youth and gang violence. At Larkins I was pumped for what I knew. I told them that many in the gangs lived in the streets around me, and that I had gone to school with them. The Guvnors hadn't been directly involved in the murder, as it happened, but I took some photographs of them into the office, where I was told I should try to get them published. Someone suggested taking them to *The Observer*, a liberal, socially concerned quality Sunday newspaper which I had never read.

In those days there was none of the sophisticated security apparatus that now bars newspaper doors. In my hopsack suit and suedes, I was able to walk straight into *The Observer* offices in Tudor Street and be directed to the picture desk without prior appointment. The picture editor, a man called Cliff Hopkinson, looked carefully through my folder, then swung back in his chair and gave me a long inquisitive look.

'Did you take these?' he said at last.

'Yes,' was all I replied.

He said, 'I like the picture, and I'm going to use it. Would you do some more for me?'

I left, full of excitement, with a formal commission for more pictures, and a writer by the name of Clancy Sigal was asked to produce the story. Yet Finsbury Park was still to have its say in the matter.

Even as I was leaving the cafe in Blackstock Road, at the end of the session photographing the boys, I saw the familiar Wolseley waiting. As I approached, the car door opened and I heard the friendly invitation from the law.

'Get in.'

I said, 'No.'

'Get in if you know what's good for you.'

I got in. Always resist the first time, but never take it too far. That was the game around here.

'We've reason to believe that you have been in that cafe with a stolen camera.'

I told them it was not stolen. They asked to see the purchase receipt, which of course I didn't have with me. They suggested a short drive to where I lived to find the receipt, otherwise I'd be heading straight for the police station.

'Okay,' I said, 'but do me a favour – don't park outside my house. If my mother sees you, you'll be in terrible trouble.'

That broke them up: 'So your mother is tough, eh?' but they did as I asked. I went in the house, rummaged through my little chest of drawers and found the receipt. When the old lady asked what I was doing I just said that I was tidying up. When I nipped out to show the receipt to the police they went all oily.

'Can we drop you back to where we first found you, sir?'

It was a wonderful moment, refusing a copper's favour and seeing them off. And of course I really had been of assistance to the law. If my mother had come across them harassing me over the camera, there is no question, she would have brained them with the heaviest available ornament.

The pictures were published as a half page in *The Observer* on 15 February 1959. I was 23 years old. The big picture was one I had taken before the killing. It showed the lads in their best suits posed in a burned-out house in The Bunk, though it had been renamed Wadcote Street to improve its image. I had got them together as they were setting off for an afternoon at the Astoria cinema.

Now, much more than then, I can recognize that it was a strong picture. It shows an awareness of structure that must have been instinctive because I would not have known what the term meant at the time. It was also brilliantly exposed, which must have been a fluke, for I did not possess a light meter.

That one picture changed my life. People have told me that if I had not made a breakthrough with that photograph, then I would have done so with another. I don't think that would necessarily have been the case. I had a low tolerance of rejection, and no burning desire to be a photographer. If I had been obliged to battle my way into Fleet Street, I would never have got there.

1990

An Interview with Kate Adie

In 1989, The BBC's Special Assignment reporter, Kate Adie, took part in this interview with students at Framingham Earl County High School in Norwich. What follows is a direct transcript of part of the interview.

Interviewer: When you were reporting from Libya, how did you ensure that you didn't get emotionally involved?

Kate Adie: One of the rules for any reporter is not to get emotionally involved, and at times it's very, very difficult. For example, if you go to a disaster or where someone's been killed and you meet people who are in a terrible state themselves, or you see something which moves you so much, you think it's natural, isn't it, to express sympathy or to want to feel like those people do; it's the normal thing, and all reporters have to guard against it because what you say to yourself first of all is the reason I'm here is not to break down in tears, or even to help; the reason I've been sent is because I have a professional job and I'm here to report. That's the only reason you've got, so you have to, to a certain extent, set your feelings aside. Some people sometimes confuse that with being hard. They say if you go round all these places, you don't have any feelings for it after a bit, you're different. Well, you must try never to be like that... but when you go to something, your feelings come very far down the line in any priorities and they mustn't get into your report.

I on one or two occasions have heard criticism of me saying, 'Oh well, because she's a woman, you know, it was an emotional report.' I'm going to say something: I defy anyone to find the emotion in my reports. One of the single things I do, simply, is that my reports very rarely have adjectives in them. I know when everyone writes essays in schools, they always say, 'Come on, use some adjectives, give it some colour, give it some feeling, try and describe things.' Well, one of the things you often do with reporting is not to put adjectives in.

Interviewer: Do you think it's justified to interview bereaved people? It can do them quite a lot of emotional harm, I should think.

Kate Adie Reporters should never intrude where it's going to be hurtful, where it's going to be distressing to people, and where there are absolutely no grounds for going in – particularly where something is very, very private. On the other hand, having said that, there are matters of public importance where it is necessary, in the view of reporters, to get over some information. Now, this does not mean going up to bereaved people and saying, 'How do you feel?' That is totally unjustified. On the other hand, there are a number of occasions, a number of circumstances where reporters do ask questions and people who are watching are a bit worried, and sometimes I think those worries are a little unfounded. For example, I've been to a number of accidents where people have been in a bit of a state afterwards – you must never interview people when they're in shock; that's very important and it's not always easy to recognize that people are in shock. But there are people who have experienced sometimes very dramatic and very frightening things or very upsetting things, and they want to talk to you.

One of the problems we have as British people is that we have a stiff upper lip and we don't actually talk to each other, and we don't talk to each other about emotional things. Come on, you've all known it: somebody's in a terrible state, crying perhaps, particularly if it's a boy. It's embarrassing, isn't it? We don't actually go and ask questions; we just sort of keep ourselves to ourselves. As a nation we do that tremendously, and sometimes people are only too desirous – they want to tell someone what happened. They *want* to. Now you might say that television or radio is not the right place to do that, but a reporter has to judge that and make sure that it's not taking advantage of anyone or being unfair or intrusive. But at the same time I have interviewed many people who have said, 'Do you know, I wanted to tell someone and no one would listen to me, 'cos they're all a bit embarrassed.'

You must also never intrude in the way of asking questions where people are not capable of judging or making the right judgement. For example, as I've said, if they're in shock, or if they really don't know what has happened around them. Quite a lot of people, for example, who were involved in major disasters or very shocking events don't know there and then what's happened around them – they may not know that dozens and dozens of people may have been hurt. They often don't know. And therefore, again, it's unfair to ask them questions because they don't know really what's been going on.

Interviewer: You've seen things which have upset you. Do you take things home? Does it give you a different outlook?

Kate Adie: Oh yes, it makes you feel very strongly. Any reporter who goes through life without actually being affected by what they see might as well give up there and then. It really means that they're not very sensitive people and I think all reporters should be sensitive. Yes – I feel very strongly about some things that I see. I'll give you a very straightforward example. I've been to one or two accidents and I've wondered myself how people can help better...

I went to the Zeebrugge ferry disaster. One of the most impressive things about that was the number of young people who helped. They were all members of the Belgian Red Cross. The average member of the Belgian Red Cross is aged between 17, I think, and 23. It's the big trendy thing to do; everybody wants to join it, because it's incredibly important, and everybody who actually helps with the Red Cross says that the sort of things the Red Cross do, particularly in Belgium, is helping at major disasters, and all the young people are given responsibility – they are asked to do it. They all have two-way radios. They are all taught to drive. And they're all told, this is your responsibility – to set up radio communications, to help with survivors, to go round the hospitals and take messages, to get phone calls through to people back in England where people were desperate for information. These young people were told: this is your job...

Interviewer: So you do sometimes have some influence, try to have some influence, over the general public in things which you couldn't really be accused of being biased in?

Kate Adie: I think you have to be very careful. I suppose everybody should say that as a reporter you should try to influence for the good. But, now look, what's the good? Is the good what a government says? Is the good what a church says? Is the good what your parents say? Is the good what your teachers say? Or is the good what you say? I am not a person to be able to define that...

The other thing that a reporter's involved with infuencing people about is purely to say – and it's a very, very basic reason why I do the job and so do my colleagues – people ought to know. Information is more important than ignorance. Education is more important than indifference. That's very fundamental and hiding things is very often wrong...

If you look at a newspaper, do you read all the stories?

Interviewer: No.

Kate Adie: But it's all going on, isn't it? So you are selecting, aren't you, things you find interesting. And at the same time if a story is quite interesting for a few days, along comes something else and – oh well – you read that instead or listen to something about that. We've all got rather short attention spans these days, and television news is part of that. I find myself, in the ten years I've been a television reporter, that we are spending a shorter and shorter time on every story now. Partly that's because we can go to more places and bring more news of different places and different people and different events – and there's only so much you can put on a screen. And at the same time we are ourselves very worried about the fact that people think, 'Oh look, it's that again' because they're treating news as a form of entertainment. And after the same old story, you want a new story...

Interviewer: Picking up your point about entertainment, do you consider that tabloid papers should be called newspapers?

Kate Adie: I think that most of the tabloid papers in this country now are not very 'newsy'. I don't think they are about news and information and – this is a personal opinion – I think this has happened in the last few years. Whether it changes, I've no idea. Again, what you have to say is, what is news? A lot of people don't read about the more serious things in life – the politics, the economics, the finance, all those sorts of things. At the same time, we have now got a lot of tabloid newspapers which are not reporting news. Quite a number of them, they don't invent it, but they decide what they're going to pursue – in other words they say isn't it time we had a story about a pop star and a drugs scandal, and they tend to sniff around for that sort of thing. Now that's not straightforward news, and there's quite a lot of that goes on – what you could call 'creative writing' rather than reporting...

Interviewer: Do you think the papers use too much loaded language, say as political propaganda?'

Kate Adie: I do think what happens is not so much loaded language; I think there is extremely violent language used in reporting these days, which is absolutely unjustified. Politicians are always having 'fights', people are always 'struggling'; people are always being 'blasted'; people are always 'hitting back'. I think this is appalling. I think the language of violence that's used to describe perfectly ordinary arguments, disagreements, different points of view is an extremely poor use of language in nearly all our reporting these days. I think language is far too violent.

Interviewer: If, when you were starting out as a reporter, you were offered a good job on a tabloid newspaper, would you have taken it?

Kate Adie: I don't think so. I don't think I would want to write for such a newspaper. I've never written for a newspaper – I've always been either in radio or television – so I'm not actually qualified. I don't think they would have offered me a job. I'll tell you one of the differences which I wouldn't have liked. In newspapers there's an editorial system, as there is in radio and television. But in newspapers it's considerably different. In newspapers nearly all reporters have their copy rewritten. 'Copy' is the word for the words they put down on a site and when they write their story... Their copy is usually edited. First of all it's edited to fit in to the amount of space the newspaper is going to give that story. Secondly it's often edited to fit the style of the newspaper. As we've said, it's a matter of language – the kinds of long words in some newspapers, short words in others and also the kind of style of the newspaper, the way it reads. And thirdly, it's often changed to fit the view of the newspaper, the political view or the stance it is taking on something.

Television and radio has much, much less of this. It has an editorial process – in other words, your reports come in. But in radio and television they are much more likely to stand as the original reporter's words, in radio, and the words and the pictures, in television, without much change, if any, coming from the senior editors. It's a much more direct kind of reporting, which to me makes it much more satisfying as a job, because what you do on site, out wherever you are, is what goes out on air. There is an editorial process and if your editor thinks you've got it wrong, or he thinks that you are inaccurate, or he thinks that the style is inappropriate, or he thinks there are facts which aren't checked in it, he can change it, or he can drop the item, or he can have it revoiced back in the building. But on the whole, what you are paid for, as a reporter in radio and television, is to be able to get your facts right and to get it as an acceptable story from where you are doing it. So there's a big difference between the two sorts of reporting in newspapers and the media.

1989

Following the Shining Path

John Simpson

MARTYN (INSET: PERU)
Mon Oct 26 21:24 1992

MARTYN[1] IN VISION	Peru's ruthless guerilla group, the Shining Path, is continuing its campaign of murder and oppression, despite the capture and imprisonment of its leader last month. Abimael Guzman, who believes he can create a Maoist state through violence, was seized and jailed by the Government last month. Our Foreign Affairs Editor, John Simpson, has been to the shanty towns of Peru, where people fear Guzman's arrest has strengthened the hand of the hardliners, putting the
VT[2] FOLLOWS	country on the verge of dictatorship.

VT (2′ 42″)
IN WORDS: 'The vast shanty towns ...'
OUT WORDS: '.... BBC News, Lima.'
2′ 24″ (VT)

JOHN SIMPSON: The vast shanty towns of Lima are harsh and barren; there are no social services here, no policing, no water, no electricity unless the local people fix it up. The Government ignores them, and the vacuum has partly been filled by the Shining Path Movement, which is by no means out of business.

1 Martyn Lewis, the newscaster
2 VT = Videotape

The funeral the other day of a couple and two of their sons, petty crooks, one of whom was stupid enough to rob a Shining Path official. The Shining Path came back and wiped out everyone in the house over the age of twelve. The organization kills brutally and for maximum effect. People in the inaptly named Villa Himosa, meaning beautiful town, won't quickly offend the Shining Path again.

The Government has been making a deliberate effort to humiliate the movement's founder and inspiration, Abimael Guzman, displaying him as a caged animal. Shining Path is now without an effective head. Its supporters are as intensely dedicated as ever but they've lost his strategic skills, which many Peruvian politicians had feared would sooner or later lead the Shining Path to overthrow the State and form its own Maoist Government in Peru.

The army has moved in to take heavy advantage of Guzman's fall, there've been big sweeps in the shanty towns. Things have changed from the days when Shining Path achieved its remarkable success because the Government forces had lost their morale and seemed so feeble. Shining Path was cleverer and more successful.

For the people of the shanty towns now, the army operations are terrifying. These men were arrested for not having documents; the army says that makes them suspected terrorists. That's led to torture and death before now.

An angry crowd gathered, fearful for the fate of the arrested men, one woman had brought her son's documents, it made no difference, her son was taken away. In the battle against Shining Path few hearts and minds were won. The Shining Path is as highly disciplined as any revolutionary movement in history; it certainly isn't going to fall apart now that its chief source of inspiration has been cut off for life. Its next opportunity to show its strength will be the elections here at the end of next month, only then will we know if Shining Path can reproduce its old ferocity. John Simpson, BBC News, Lima.

26 October 1992

The New Journalism: Law and Lawlessness

The New Journalism

Tom Wolfe

...If you follow the progress of the New Journalism closely through the 1960s, you see an interesting thing happening. You see journalists learning the techniques of realism – particularly of the sort found in Fielding, Smollett, Balzac, Dickens and Gogol – from scratch. By trial and error, by 'instinct' rather than theory, journalists began to discover the devices that gave the realistic novel its unique power, variously known as its 'immediacy', its 'concrete reality', its 'emotional involvement', its 'gripping' or 'absorbing' quality.

This extraordinary power was derived mainly from just four devices, they discovered. The basic one was scene-by-scene construction, telling the story by moving from scene to scene and resorting as little as possible to sheer historical narrative. Hence the sometimes extraordinary feats of reporting that the new journalists undertook: so that they could actually witness the scenes in other people's lives as they took place – and record the dialogue in full, which was device number two. Magazine writers, like the early novelists, learned by trial and error something that has since been demonstrated in academic studies: namely, that realistic dialogue involves the reader more completely than any other single device. It also establishes and defines character more quickly and effectively than any other single device. (Dickens has a way of fixing a character in your mind so that you have the feeling he has described every inch of his appearance – only to go back and discover that he actually took care of the physical description in two or three sentences; the rest he has accomplished with dialogue.) Journalists were working on dialogue of the fullest, most completely revealing sort in the very moment when novelists were cutting back, using dialogue in more and more cryptic, fey and curiously abstract ways.

The third device was the so-called 'third person point of view', the technique of presenting every scene to the reader through the eyes of a particular character, giving the reader the feeling of being inside the character's mind and experiencing the emotional reality of the scene as he experiences it. Journalists had often used the first person point of view – 'I was there' – just as autobiographers, memoirists and novelists had. This is very limiting for the journalist, however, since he can bring the reader inside the mind of only one character – himself – a point of view that often proves irrelevant to the story and irritating to the reader. Yet how could a journalist, writing non-fiction, accurately penetrate the thoughts of another person?

The answer proved to be marvellously simple: interview him about his thoughts and emotions, along with everything else. This was what I had done in *The Electric Kool-Aid Acid Test*, what John Sack did in *M* and what Gay Talese did in *Honour Thy Father*.

The fourth device has always been the least understood. This is the recording of everyday gestures, habits, manners, customs, styles of furniture, clothing, decorations, styles of travelling, eating, keeping house, modes of behaving towards children, servants, superiors, inferiors, peers, plus the various looks, glances, poses, styles of walking and other symbolic details that might exist within a scene. Symbolic of what? Symbolic, generally, of people's *status life*, using the term in the broad sense of the entire pattern of behaviour and possessions through which people express their position in the world or what they think it is or what they hope it to be. The recording of such details is not mere embroidery in prose. It lies as close to the centre of the power of realism as any other device in literature...

1972

The Detective

James Mills

Looking south into the chaos of his precinct, Barrett says, 'This is a fast track, and if you can't stay in the ball game you get farmed out. If you're a little old lady detective, you end up in a little old lady precinct, out in Queens. Over 20,000 guys in uniform want to be detectives, because they want the title, "Detective," and they think they'd like this job – "Broadway Detective," very glamorous.'

Barrett works in a 'block' of four men. They take turns 'catching squeals' (recording and investigating complaints). This evening two of his partners are back in the station house typing out reports and answering phones, while Barrett, who types fast and would rather be on the street, patrols with the fourth partner. Barrett says that he feels 'ambitious', but he wants to be particularly selective tonight about making an arrest because his 'swing' (days off) begins tomorrow. If he makes an arrest tonight he will have to spend tomorrow in court on his own time, extending his workday to more than 20 straight hours. So he is going to be selective. But there are ways to discourage crime without going to court.

Barrett has walked less than a block when he and his partner stop next to a parking lot and stand there casually continuing their conversation about the New York Giants. Neither has mentioned it to the other, but both have spotted a tall, thin man who started into the empty attendant's shack in the parking lot, then quickly backed out when he saw the attendant looking at him from the lot. Now the thin man walks past them, and they resume their stroll, watching him. He moves fast, looking in cars as he hurries by them. He is down to 47th and Broadway when he stops short at a car, peers in and opens the door. He reaches into the car and comes out with a toy camera which he shakes, listens to and tosses into a trash can. 'That's petty larcency, no matter what the thing's worth,' Barrett says, 'but let's see what develops.' The man eyes sidewalk merchandise, goes in a drugstore and cases the counters. Finally he is coming out of a clothing store with his hands full of ties and Barrett grabs him.

'Hey, man, what you doin' to me, why you grabbin' me, I'm gonna pay for them, I was gonna pay.'

Barrett and his partner take the man back into the store and find the manager, who says he is being robbed blind and will definitely go to court as a complainant. The thief is making a fuss, playing to a crowd of shoppers. 'I'll pay for the ties, man. Let me go home and I'll be good. I promise, man. I'll be good. I wouldn't lie to you.'

'You wouldn't lie,' Barrett says. 'No, you wouldn't lie. What about the toy camera?'

'What toy camera?'

'The one you took out of the car.'

'What car?'

Barrett and his partner take the man to the station house and up the antique spiral staircase to the squad room. The five-storey brick building – often condemned but never vacated – has been there since the Civil War. Its scarred walls are flaking off their millionth coat of paint, and the thick wooden floors creak with the burdens of a century. They walk past a small wooden bench for waiting complainants through a waist-high steel swinging gate with a broken latch. Barrett tells the prisoner to sit down and he settles into a broken wooden chair tied together with twine. The five desks are scarred and ancient, one of them steadied with a quarter-inch stack of arrest cards under a short leg. Wastebaskets overflow onto the tobacco-brown floor, littered with discarded forms, cigarette butts, rubber bands and pins that serve for paper clips. Light comes from four ceiling lamps – the broken globe on one has been replaced with a piece of bent cardboard. The green walls are covered with framed pictures of the FBI's ten most wanted criminals, and smaller shots of teenage boys and girls who have run away from home to seek the glamour of Times Square (some of them go home after the first taste, other end up as drug addicts or prostitutes).

A wire cage the size of a large closet contains four prisoners in one corner of the room. Three are drug addicts arrested for boosting cars and one is a female impersonator loudly demanding to be separated from 'such riffraff'. A blind boy is explaining to a detective at a desk how someone walked up to him on Seventh Avenue, grabbed the wallet out of his pocket and ran. At another desk a man, his wife and her sister are reporting a burglary, all of them talking at once.

A detective questions a 25-year-old A and R man arrested for attacking a passer-by with a knife on 48th Street. 'What's your name?' he asks.

'Who, me?' The prisoner is a pro at countering interrogation.

'Yeah, you. What's your name?'

'My name?'

'Your name. What's your name?'

'My name's Sonny.'

'What's your last name?'

'My last name?'

'Look! What's your name, all of it?'

'Sonny Davis.'

'Where do you live?'

'Where do I live?'

It goes on like that, and Barrett looks disgusted. He does not interfere, but he would not have put up with it. He is a good interrogator and he knows that you do not get anywhere with a prisoner until you break down the barrier between his world and yours. You are neatly dressed, relaxed, secure, educated and a cop. He is shabby, nervous, defiant and a prisoner. There is no communication until by a soft word, a tough word, a cigarette, a slap in the face – depending on the individual – the gap is bridged and real talk begins.

1965

In Search of the Cocaine Pirates

P. J. O'Rourke

A headline caught my eye: CARIBBEAN ISLANDS' TOP OFFICIALS HELD IN DRUG SMUGGLING PLOT. It seemed that on March 6, 1985, in a Miami Ramada Inn, the Drug Enforcement Agency had arrested Norman Saunders, the Chief Minister and Head of State of a British Crown Colony called the Turks and Caicos Island. Saunders was videotaped stuffing $20,000 into his pants pockets. He and two other officials from the islands' 11-member Parliament – Minister of Commerce and Development Stafford Missick and legislator Aulden 'Smokey' Smith – were charged with 17 counts of conspiracy to smuggle narcotics. Thus, at day's end, 27 per cent of the Turks and Caicos elected Government was cooling its heels in a US slammer.

That was more like it. No national magazine had done a story about drug smuggling in the Caribbean for, I don't know, a week. I could fly to the Turks and Caicos in between chats with fiduciary nabobs and get trouble plenty.

Nor was this the first spore of dark narco evil to come whiffing out of these airstrip-dotted, many harboured cays at the remote southeastern reach of the Bahamas chain. We journalists keep up on such things. For years the English press had been running articles like PARADISE FOR PEDLARS – ISLAND COLONY KEY TO A MULTIMILLION DRUG TRADE (*Daily Express*, September 7, 1982). The London *Times* said that in the late seventies 'law enforcement officials reckoned that 90 per cent[!] of the marijuana entering the United States was being moved through the Turks and Caicos.' *The Sunday Telegraph* warned, 'Narcotics money is so influential that it is rapidly bringing about the creation of a completely new power structure in the Turks, a whole new political system.'

I checked the Saunders story in various newspapers. Apparently the Turks and Caicos natives were not grateful for the DEA's efforts. 'Talk of retribution, of hostages... and of British warships rushing to the scene' was reported by *The Washington Post* under the front page headline DRUG ARRESTS RAISE ISLANDS' TENSION – BRITISH GOVERNOR URGES POPULACE NOT 'TO TAKE TO THE STREETS'. *The New York Times* said the new acting chief minister, Mr Nathaniel 'Bops' Francis, 'declared indignantly that Mr Saunders was "framed" and he spoke angrily of a racist plot hatched by white Americans.' 'Aftershocks... rumbled through the eight-isle British territory,' read the lead on a *Miami Herald* story which quoted the Commerce Minister's nephew as saying, 'It's not a disgrace that they were interested in money. It is a disgrace that they got caught.' And what kind of country has Members of Parliament with names like Bops and Smokey, anyway? The place must be a new pirate republic.

There were a number of these in the Caribbean, Tortuga being the most famous. It was colonized in the 1600s by a group of French buccaneers called the Coast Brotherhood. They preyed on the Spanish plate fleet (and anything else). Another freebooter mini-nation was New Providence, on the site of modern Nassau. Founded in 1716, it counted among its citizens 'Calico Jack' Rackham and Edward 'Blackbeard' Teach. Rackham was famous for wearing lightweight cotton clothing, Blackbeard for setting off firecrackers in his beard and drinking rum and gunpowder. They robbed ships and killed people too. The Head of State in New Providence was a half-mad castaway the pirates found on the beach. They styled him 'Governor' and made up elaborate official protocols.

The Turks and Caicos would be up-to-date, of course. There'd be no Jolly Rogers on the big Herreshoff yachts, just Colombian registries. Sinister black cigarette speedboats would be bobbing at the docks, no doubt, Learjets lurking under camoflage nets, big *campesinos* in Armani suits fingering their Uzis and MAC-10s while Guajira Peninsula warlords gestured grandly to scruffy Americans with Rolex watches. And, naturally, there would be tow-haired, Hershey-tanned, near-naked dope-dealer girlfriends everywhere – bodies hard, eyes hard too. Plus bartops slathered with fine-chopped pink-auraed Andean flake pushed into lines thick as biceps.

What to pack? Swim suit, flip-flops, .357 magnum... On the other hand, given the Latin blow vendors' penchant for murdering wives, infants, not to mention writers, maybe a note from my doctor about taking a sunshine psoriasis cure. The travel brochures made prominent mention of bank secrecy laws, I noticed. The Third Turtle Inn on the island of Providenciales seemed to be the first-rate place to stay. I hit on a cautious, neutral sort of disguise: summer-weight blue blazer, chinos, and deck shoes – a bit lawyerish, a touch bankery, just a South Florida yuppie, you know, just brushing shoulders with the scene, in for a little sit-down with at client maybe or bundling some fungibles through a corporate shell. Businesslike, that is, but not *undercover*, for God's sake, or nosy or *too* businesslike. I flew in from Miami. The sweltering tin-roofed airport, the too-casual customs agents, the thornbush-and-palm-scrub landscape all breathed menace. I went to the bar at the Third Turtle, ordered a gin – 'Make that a double' – lit a cigarette, and looked knowing.

'Jesus Christ,' said somebody in the bar, 'another newspaper reporter. How come all you guys wear blue blazers? Is it a *club* or what?'

'Uh,' I said. 'Er... oh... I'll bet folks around here are pretty upset about Noman Saunders and everybody getting arrested in Miami,' I said, subtly turning the subject towards drugs.

'Upset?!' said someone else, 'Goddam right we're upset. Norman and Smokey are the two best tennis players in the islands, and the tournament is *next week*!'

Perhaps this wasn't exactly the story I thought.

The Turks and Caicos rope through eighty miles of ocean. They are outcroppings of eolian limestone, piles of fossil seashell bits, really. There are a few hills, but mostly the islands are near sea level or at it. Mangrove tangles fill the low spots. On first glance, as tropical paradises go, the Ts and Cs are sort of like the roof of your apartment building. Rainfall is scant, topsoil rare. Nice beaches, though, and the wind and water carve the soft rock into rococo shorelines and mysterious sea caves and startling sinkholes fit for Aztec maiden sacrifices. The people are hopelessly friendly. I had to trade in my rented scooter for a Jeep because of so much waving. You don't want to take a hand off the handlebars on what passes for a road down there. A few hundred yards from shore are splendid coral reefs poised on the edge of 'the wall', the thousand-metre dropoff at the end of the continental shelf. It's a good place to scuba-dive (or, I mused hopefully, lose a competitor wearing cement Top-Siders). The vegetation is low, harsh, and tangled, but it goes on for miles without human interruption, some of the last truly wild land left in the North Caribbean.

There are 37 islands according to *The New York Times*, 42 according to *The Washington Post*, eight according to *The Miami Herald*. I counted 63 on the only chart I could find, which was also a placemat. Anyone in earshot – taxi drivers, fishing-boat captains, hotel maids, people standing in the road – got involved whenever I asked this question. 'East Caicos, West Caicos, North Caicos, South Caicos...' Once they started naming islands it was impossible to stop them. '...and Middle Caicos and Providenciales and Pine Cay and Grand Turk and Guana Cay and Nigger Cay but we don't call it that anymore and Back Cay and French Cay, Bush Cay, Fish Cays, Big Ambergris, Little Ambergris... wait, now, do you mean high tide or low?'

Only 8500 people live on only six of those islands. Almost as many more are in the Bahamas, Britain, the United States, or somewhere else they can find jobs.

Every spring in the Turks and Caicos there's a hatch of handsome black handspan-sized Erebus moths. They're called 'money bats'. If they land on you it's said they bring fortune. Obviously they don't bring much. The locals work at conch diving, lobster fishing, a few tourism jobs – there's not a lot to do for a living. In fact, there's not a lot to do.

I interviewed the British governor, the opposition leader, and (the arrested people having politely resigned) the new Chief

Minister and the new Minister of Commerce, Development, and Tourism.

Nobody had a bad word, or even an enlightening one, to say about former Chief Minister Norman Saunders. He's personable, generous, easy to work with. He's handsome and a tasteful dresser as well. On his home island of South Caicos he commands special affection. His picture is all over the place above a political slogan that sound like rejected name ideas from *Snow White and the Seven Dwarves*: 'Firm, Frank, Friendly, Faithful'. I was counting on an earful from opposition leader Clement Howell. But they've only had party politics in the Turks and Caicos since 1975, and as yet they seem politely confused about what to do with them...

1987

Among the Thugs

Bill Buford

Some time ago, I came home from Wales by train. The station was a village station just outside Cardiff, and I arrived early. I bought a cup of tea. It was a cold Saturday evening, and only three or four other passengers were on the platform. A man was reading a newspaper, rocking back and forth on his feet. We waited, and there was an announcement on the loudspeaker about an unscheduled train. A little later, there was another announcement: the unscheduled train was about to appear, and everyone was to stand ten feet from the edge of the platform. It was an unusual instruction, and the man with the newspaper raised an eyebrow. Perhaps, I thought, it was a military train of some kind. A few minutes later, police appeared, emerging from the stairs nearby.

The train was a football special, and it had been taken over by supporters. They were from Liverpool, and there were hundreds of them – I had never seen a train with so many people inside – and they were singing in unison: 'Liverpool, la la la, Liverpool, la la la.' The words look silly now, but they did not sound silly. A minute before there had been virtual silence: a misty, sleepy Welsh winter evening. And then this song, pounded out with increasing ferocity, echoing off the walls of the station. A guard had been injured, and as the train stopped he was rushed off, holding his face. Someone inside was trying to smash a window with a table leg, but the window wouldn't break. A fat man with a red face stumbled out of one of the carriages, and six policemen rushed up to him, wrestled him to the ground and bent his arm violently behind his back. The police were overreacting – the train was so packed that the fat man had popped out of an open door – but the police were frightened. For that matter, I was frightened (I remember my arms folded stupidly across my chest), as was everyone else on the platform. It was peculiar: I was at a railway station where everyone around me spoke Welsh; I was there to catch a train: then this sudden display. I thought that it was intended for us, that this violent chant was a way of telling us that they, the supporters, were in the position to do anything they wanted.

The train left. It was silent.

I got home at one-thirty in the morning, and the country seemed to consist of a long cordon of police. At Paddington Station 200 officers were waiting to escort everyone from the platform to the Underground. I changed trains four times; three were taken over by supporters. One was torn apart: the seats had been ripped out, and the bar, which had been closed beforehand, was broken up, its metal shutter-door split into pieces and drink handed out to anyone who walked past. I did not know what was more surprising, the destructiveness, which was gratuitous and relentless, or that, with so many police, no one seemed able to stop it: it just went on. Hoping to avoid trouble, I sat in a first-class carriage at the very front of one train, opposite a man who had paid for his first-class ticket. He was a slim, elegant man with a thin moustache, wearing a woollen suit and expensive, shiny shoes: a civilized sort of fellow reading a civilized sort of book – a hardback novel with a dust-jacket. A supporter had been staring at him for a long time. The supporter was drunk. Every now and then, he lit a match and threw it at the civilized man's shiny shoes, hoping to set his trousers on fire. The civilized man ignored him, but the supporter, puffy and bloodshot, persisted. It was a telling image: one of the disenfranchised, flouting the codes of civilized conduct, casually setting a member of a more privileged class alight.

It was obvious that the violence was a protest. It made sense that it would be: that football matches were providing an outlet for frustrations of a powerful nature. So many young people were out of work or had never been able to find any. The violence, it followed, was a rebellion of some kind – social rebellion, class rebellion, something. I wanted to know more. I had read about the violence and, to the extent that I thought about it, had assumed that it was an isolated thing or mysterious in the way that crowd violence is meant to be mysterious: unpredictable, spontaneous, the mob. My journey from Wales suggested that it might be more intended, more willed. It offered up a vision of the English Saturday, the shopping day, that was different from the one I had known: that in the towns and cities, you might find hundreds of police, military in their comprehensiveness, out to contain young, male sports fans who, after attending an athletic contest, were determined to break or destroy the things that were in their way. It was hard to believe.

I repeated the story of my journey to friends, but I was surprised by how unsurprised they were. Some acted as if they were disgusted; other were amused; no one thought it was anything extraordinary. It was one of the things you put up with: that every Saturday young males trashed your trains, broke the windows of your pubs, destroyed your cars, wreaked havoc on your town centres. I didn't buy it, but it seemed to be so. In fact the only time I felt I had said something surprising was when I revealed that, although I had now seen a football crowd, I had never been to an English football match. This, it seemed, was shocking...

1991

What you Get when you Cross a Chicken with a Rottweiler

William Leith

TUESDAY The guy who breeds Rottweilers says: 'Well, I really don't know... we've had such a lot of trouble with you people.'

'But I'm not going to say all that stuff...'

'No, honestly. You'll just go on about how vicious and terrifying the dogs are. I mean, unless you really know about dogs...'

'But I do.'

'You do?'

'Oh yes,' I say, sensing victory. 'I mean, Rottweilers are... I really, uh, like them.'

'They don't scare you, then?'

'Scare me?' I laugh, fairly convincingly.

Two minutes later I put the phone down. It's on.

THURSDAY I'm driving along, thinking: there's no reason I should give myself away. The dogs will be in cages. I'll just keep calm, maybe stroke one on the head or something. Just look competent. I pull into the drive of the guy's farm in the country; he's waiting for me at the gateway. I park, get out of the car, walk across the gravel drive, looking for the dogs, pretending not to.

'Nice to see you.'

'Yes. How many, uh, how many ...Rottweil... ' I clear my throat. 'How many actual... dogs do you have here?'

'You mean fully grown?'

'What? Yes...'

'Thirty. Thirty-two, actually.'

'And... where are they?'

'Where are they? All over, really. Don't worry, you'll get a chance to see all of them.'

'Ah, That's good.' We walk towards the farmhouse. I can hear loud noises coming from behind the building: barking, growling.

'So. The dogs are over here, then, eh?' I'm being too chatty here, I know, with this square-jawed wiry guy in a Barbour Thornproof. He possibly talks to dogs more then he does to humans. The barking is louder now, and there's something else; a scraping, a scrabbling. Claws. We turn a corner into a courtyard; around the edge are coops and runs. Inside are the dogs. It's difficult to describe them. They're just huge man-sized slabs of muscle: Mike Tyson with jaws like garden shears. The guy points. I smile.

'Nice, uh, dogs.' He looks at me, looks back again, says nothing. I nod and clench my jaw in the way I imagine a dog-breeding enthusiast would. I think: I have to show him some sign that I'm not frightened. But what? I'll have to go nearer the cages. I walk towards them, looking at the ground, trying not to catch the eye of the dogs. I can see the large loping black shapes quicken in their movements; I'm exciting them, stirring something up deep in their backward little brains. But they're in cages! They can't touch me. Now I'm a yard away. Nothing can...

'Whooah!' I leap back; an electric shock has passed through me, I'm shaking with fear, fear has made me neurologically unstable, I'm fighting for breath. The man looks at me.

'Just... hah! Just a little, whew! Surprised, that's... that's all.'

'Shall we go inside?'

We walk towards the house, me aware that I'm on my last chance, him saying nothing. We crunch across the gravel. My legs are shaking.

I say: 'Powerful dogs, eh?' He looks at me, shakes his head.

'Do you want a coffee?'

'Yes... '

'Or a cup of tea?'

'Yes.'

'Well... which do you want?'

'Either. Is that all the dogs, then?'

'No, we've got a few more. Why?'

'Why? Because... I'm interested to see them, you know. Are there any in the house?'

'Oh, yes.'

He opens the porch door. He looks like he's just about tolerating me. I say: 'Look, I'm sorry about before...' He walks on ahead of me, into the kitchen, and sits down.

And then I can hear it, a few yards away still, out of sight, the scrabbling, the noises of a huge frantic animal, and I'm going to try to keep calm, now's my chance. It bursts into the room, about fifteen stone, six feet long, heading for me of course, but I'm doing fine, I'll just keep entirely still, and I don't know why, but suddenly I'm against the wall, screaming, the dog pinning me to the wall by the chest, the huge head slapping against mine, tongue, teeth right up against my face, my arms up above my head, surrendering.

'Aaaroooaw! No! No! AAAH! It's, it's, ah! No!'

'Put your hands down! Put them down!'

'No! No!'

'Put them down, for Christ's sake!'

'But he'll... '

'Don't you know anything? That's *why* he's...'

'I can't, I can't!' I'm thinking: he's mauling me, but no blood yet, no jaws clamping, ripping me up. I can see what the man is saying. He's telling me that if I put my hands down, the dog will stop. I lower my right hand, clenched in a fist. Nothing much happens. Then I lower my left hand. The dog, after a second or two more of nearly biting my head off, but apparently not doing so, gets down.

'You mustn't put your hands up like that.'

'Of course,' I say, shaking my head, panting. 'Of course.'

Five minutes later I'm sitting at the table, tea in front of me, shaking so little now that I'll soon be able to pick the cup up, perhaps even before it's gone cold. The dog-breeder's wife has joined us. She says: 'So – you know a bit about dogs, do you?'

'I, I, there's, ooh! Aah!' There's something under the table, and it's going for my leg. I move back, fast, backing away, the chair falling with a crash. It's a pug, a horrid little thing with bug-eyes, nosing around at my feet. I pick up the chair, slowly replace it. I can't think of anything to say, so I say: 'It's all right. It's only a pug.'

Then I sit down again and say: 'Well, yes. I do sort of know about dogs. Right.' And then I do the interview.

17 May 1992

Execution of the Queen of France

Her Majesty had been confined in the prison of the Conciergerie since the 1st August last, in a room twelve feet long, eight feet broad, four feet under ground, and with a grated window on a level with it. Her food was of the coarsest kind, and she was constantly kept in sight by a female prisoner and two light-horsemen. On Wednesday morning she was brought into the Court to hear her sentence. Being asked if she had anything to offer against it, she answered, 'Nothing.' Her hands were tied behind her with cords, and she was conveyed to the tumbril that waited for her. The tying her hands behind her previous to her ascending the scaffold was also a peculiar act of cruelty, not even practised on Charlotte Corday. Beside her, sat the priest and executioner. Her head was bare: the hand of the hangman had already cut off those once fair tresses. Thus attended in this constrained and painful attitude, amidst two ranks of insulting and applauding ruffians, over a rugged pavement for near a mile, passed the mother, daughter, sister, and wife of Emperors and Kings: the offspring of Maria Theresa, the descendant of the Caesars!

The procession lasted near an hour and a half; during this whole time no murmur, no sign of indignation, anger or complaint, escaped her; she looked round her with a calm and dignified air. When she mounted the scaffold, the same applauses and bravoes were heard again. She smiled. The executioners bound their victim to the plank which bowed her to the axe, and terminated all her sufferings.

The Observer, 10 November 1793

Denial of Tobacco Before Hanging

The other morning a wretched man was executed at Newgate for shooting a woman. It was not a very shocking murder, as times go: having had a quarrel with her, in a moment of frenzy he merely shot both her and himself with a revolver. Unfortunately she died, and he recovered. He was tried for murder and found guilty, with a half-and-half recommendation to mercy by the jury.

When visited in his cell by the sheriffs and the Governor a short time before his execution, he asked, it is stated, for two glasses of brandy; he also begged permission to smoke for a short time, but this request was denied. It is difficult to understand what possible objection there can be to permitting a man on the brink of death to smoke a pipe if he is so inclined. Why should he be allowed brandy, and not tobacco? In every other country but this a condemned criminal is allowed to walk to the place of execution with a pipe or cigar in his mouth. Who can tell how much the strain on the nerves in the agonizing minutes that precede death may be lessened by a few whiffs of tobacco? And even the British Anti-Tobacco Association would hardly have the heart to take the pipe out of the hands of the condemned criminal at the foot of the gallows; but officialism in England cannot relax its rules even on the edge of the grave.

The Observer, 15 December 1872

Rights of the Press at Executions

Without reflecting in any way upon the arrangements for the carrying out of the execution of Kate Webster at the Wandsworth Gaol, it is desirable that steps should be taken to prevent the Press being excluded from executions. Most people agree with the abolition of public executions. The notion of such sights acting as a deterrent to crime has long been given up as a mistake, but so long as capital punishment is allowed all executions should be carried out in the presence of independent witnesses. It is not enough that the newspapers should receive official accounts of such proceedings. There is no doubt, in case of any important personage being hung, rumours would get about that the law had been evaded, and the criminal allowed to escape. Such rumours might be unfounded, but every precaution should be taken to prevent their arising, and the best possible means of maintaining the public faith in the carrying out of such sentences is to admit the Press. All sensational reports of executions are to be deprecated, and every effort made to discourage them; but every leading newspaper should have the distinct right of sending its reporter to give the public an impartial account of the proceedings.

The Observer, 3 August 1879

Fourteen Days in May

Paul Hamann

In 1987 Paul Hamann produced a BBC documentary about the days leading up to an execution in Mississippi. The opening sequence of his documentary is presented here as a videoscript.

		U.S. RADIO STATION
0.00	Tracking shot over Mississippi River	By satellite, this is the Mississippi Network. This is the Delta's first choice for weather information – each hour with up to date weather scans, on WKCB FM stereo 95.3 – serving Crewe, Indiamola Moorhead, Alamina and the Greater Delta area. Jeff Facelly was at the State Penitentiary at Parchman today, and filed this story:
		JEFF FACELLY
		A Death Row inmate at Parchman is scheduled to die in the gas chamber in two weeks. Edward Earl Johnson was convicted of the 1979 shooting death of Walnut Grove Marshal, J.P. Crest. Johnson's attornies and the American Civil Liberties Union say they've got a strategy to save the inmate from execution on the 20 May.

0.40 Work gangs

(INMATE CALLING OUT)

INMATE 1
Ain't nothing but a game.

INMATE 2
Hey.

INMATE 1
...you all out.

INMATE 2
Get it on down.

INMATE 1
Get it back.

INMATE 2
Get it on down.

INMATE 1
Got you Brown.

INMATE 2
Did you – did you nearly talk back to me?
Go to hell man – go to hell. Now get this new...

INMATE 1
Thank you boss.

INMATE 2
I don't need that mouth.

(VEHICLE NOISE)

INMATE 1
Listen now tell me what squad this is.

INMATE 2
Eleven Hoe.

INMATE 1
What do we like to do?

INMATES
(INAUDIBLE)

INMATE 1
Tell me what we got to do?

INMATES
Get that guard.

INMATE 1
All right – what are we?

INMATES
(INAUDIBLE)

INMATE 1
What I'm talking about – snatch it all back...

INMATES
Oooh.

INMATE 1
...clean this time...

INMATE 2
Thank you – thank you sir.

		INMATE 1 Get it clean this time.
		INMATE 2 Ain't nothing but a game.
1.30	Entrance to Mississippi State Penitentiary	
1.40	'Fourteen days in May'	NARRATOR – IAN HOLM
1.45	Aerial: M.S.U.	This film is about the death penalty in the State of Mississippi, and the effect it has on the staff and inmates as time runs out for one 26-year-old man – Edward Earl Johnson. Johnson has been appealing against his sentence for eight years in the United States Courts. He was convicted in 1979 of killing a Mississippi Town Marshal, and the attempted rape of a 60-year-old woman. He has spent the last eight years on this Death Row, and has always professed his innocence.
2.20	Thursday May 27	
		DON CABANA
2.25	Ext. M.S.U.	I say we'll meet next Friday, the only thing that might er cancel that is if he receives a stay of

		DON CABANA cont'd. execution between now and then. So at this point in time the Attorney General's Office still feels very much like the execution will be a go. All of you all know, you know that could change right up to er, midnight, the twentieth.
2.45	Edward Johnson in cell	I – I got one last thing to say and then I'm going to try to – start getting ready to get out of here. I will not tolerate – one off colour remark, by anybody on this staff, about the execution.
2.55	Don Cabana	And just because I don't have to look forward to doing my job in this kind of situation doesn't mean that I can't be tolerant of others who, perhaps look forward a little more eagerly to doing it, but they can look forward to it and still do it in a professional manner. And I – er – I assure you, I've never been more serious about a threat that I've made since I've been here, if I hear anything that I don't like from staff of this Institution, they are going to answer to me directly and personally.
3.30	M.S.U: Edward out of cell	I'm sure I'll be stuck with an action later but the Personnel Department will have to clean it up and that's a promise – I – I'll get rid of 'em.

DON CABANA cont'd.
This boy's family, did not murder this police officer, this boy's family did not ask for their son to be in this situation, they didn't raise him to be in this predicament, and er, I, I've done some checking and looking into records and stuff as a matter of curiosity and this guy isn't from some family of Bo-zoes, you know. This guy represents a situation that could happen to anybody, you know you've got some heartbroken parents who've spent seven years trying to figure out what the hell went wrong.

4.15 Don Cabana: meeting cont.

We don't execute rapists and armed robbers anymore, and so when we do execute people we execute people that, that situationally anybody could find themselves in the same shoes.
You get a bad mixture of booze and bad character, or dope and booze and poor judgement and my son – your son – your daughter could end up on Death Row, any, by God, that doesn't make me bad.

4.45 Edward into exercise yard

That does not make me bad – as a parent and that means that that family's entitled to a modicum of respect from this Department and this Institution and I'm going to have it.

4.55	Don Cabana cont.	And I tell you why I'm so adament about that – because I'm concerned about some of the kind of stuff that I hear rumbling wise about people being upset about not being involved in this, that and other things – it's like I said, to Don Hocutt and a couple of others of you last night, I worry about people who are eager to stand in line – to methodically strap somebody into a chair and, and kill him.
5.20	Edward & Samuel Johnson playing chess	(BIRDS IN BACKGROUND) (LAWN MOWER) SAMUEL You playing me tough – I ain't kidding. EDWARD JOHNSON That was a good move, I think I can get that one there.

1987

Where the Law is not Blind to Colour

Antonia Swinson

'We are supposed to be vicious and cruel,' said a black inmate on Death Row, 'but this goes beyond anything we'd ever do.'

Last night's documentary *Fourteen Days in May*, (BBC1, 9.30 p.m.) recorded the final 14 days earlier this year in the life of Edward Earl Johnson, a Mississippi black man convicted on a charge of murdering a white policeman and attempted assault on a white woman.

Mistake

At 26, Edward had already been waiting to die for eight years. He was articulate from a good family – his mother is a Law Enforcement Officer – and had no previous record.

His mistake had been to sign a false confession dictated at the roadside by two white police officers.

Justice, we learned, is not colour blind.

The programme cited a recent survey which found that a black man convicted for killing a white man is four times more likely to receive the death sentence than a white man.

Then there is the problem of money.

As a Superintendent of the Penitentiary admitted, there is a different quality of justice obtained from a good private lawyer, than from a public attorney paid by the State.

If you are poor as well as black, you haven't a chance.

Where I admired – I couldn't say enjoyed – the programme so much was that the interviewer was as unobtrusive as a fly on the wall.

There was neither schmaltz nor stupid questions. The characters in this tragedy – for that is what it was – were allowed to speak for themselves.

We saw the testing of the equipment, when two black rabbits, noses still twitching, were gassed. Then there was the sad irony of Edward's mother embracing the prison staff.

Underneath it all, there was the firm belief in Edward's innocence. When his laid-back lawyer received the final news that there would be no stay of execution, he simply shrugged: 'That's the end of that.'

But to me it seemed as if that was just the beginning. Johnson died.

Next day, the Superintendent, who had earlier had 'no problem' with the prisoner's guilt, had to face the Press, and say that he had protested his innocence to the end.

The Superintendent looked shaken, and full of doubt.

Murder

Since then, a woman has come forward who says she was with Johnson on the night of the murder. She claimed she had earlier told a white Law Enforcement Officer, but had been told to mind her own business.

So how certain of a person's guilt do we have to be before they are executed?

I don't know the answer, but this magnificent programme at least had the guts to ask the question.

Daily Express, 12 November 1987

Chronicle of a Death Foretold

Thomas Sutcliffe

Waiting to be let out for exercise Edward Earl Johnson clicked his handcuffs together nervously. In a film which made you horribly sensitive to the passage of time it sounded like the ticking of a clock. Earlier, through cell bars, we had seen a close up of a cheap calender, a single day ringed in ink. If, like the prison chaplain, you had a taste for sentimental platitudes you might have called it a release date; for Johnson, his lawyer (and, as it turned out, most of the prison officers) it was the time set for an unjust killing, the day he was to be gassed for the murder of a town marshal and an attempted rape.

Paul Hamann's excellent series *The Duty Men* has already proved his ability to make gripping television out of a group of people waiting for something to happen – *Fourteen Days in May*, about the countdown to a state execution, gave that theme a desolate twist. From the beginning the film cast doubt on the validity of Johnson's conviction (he claimed his confession had been forced out of him by threats) but wisely didn't commit itself to convincing us of his innocence. Instead, by looking steadily at the routines of a bureaucratic killing, made a case against such things happening to anyone, guilty or not.

The odds were stacked against Johnson; as a black accused of killing a white policeman the lawmakers of Mississippi were not disposed in his favour. Entering one judge's chambers to make an appeal his lawyer noticed the statement of denial already on the word processor screen, waiting to be printed out. Despite such omens it was hard to believe, as you watched the warden's preparations, that sentence would really be carried out. Johnson seemed to share the sense of unreality; indeed his defence, now desperate, filed a plea of insanity based on his unnatural calm.

'The last two cases we had were stayed a day before the penalty,' the lawyer told him, 'unfortunately it's a nasty experience to get that close.' Even two weeks away was bad – the warden tested the chamber with a small black rabbit which thrashed and jerked as the cyanide vapour hit it, and then told the prisoner what he'd done. 'When he said that it gripped me, you know – they're trying it out.' It was the first of a series of moments when reality broke through an odd, dazed lack of urgency about what we were watching. As Johnson was moved to a cell closer to the gas chamber Hamann spoke haltingly to him from behind the camera and clasped his arm, running out of words of comfort but breaking the sense of distance.

As the countdown went from days to hours and then minutes you realized, with a lurch in the throat, that though the day of execution was a Wednesday, Johnson couldn't count it as part of his life – in a final indecency the sentence was to be carried out in the first minute of his last day. Just before 11.00 p.m. the Supreme Court voted against a stay and at 11.20 p.m. the Governor refused clemency. The warden, a decent man anxious for Johnson's family, spoke in solicitous, lowered tones, a parody of a bedside manner that was almost unbearable. 'We're going to get through this together', he said gently, touching Johnson's arm awkwardly. A witness who supports Johnson's alibi has since been found but there will be no retrial.

The Independent, 12 November 1987

I Live on Death Row

Michael E. Sharpe

Death Row, as I have and am experiencing it, is a reality beyond most people's imaginations.

When I was growing up into a young man, never once did it ever cross my mind that in our great country of America that we'd one day kill our own people. I know that in the old Cowboy and Indian days that life wasn't worth much. They taught me about those days in school. I heard about the old outlaw gangs and the 'bang bang, shoot 'em up, catch 'em and hang 'em days.' But I always knew that I was living in a new age. An age of new beliefs, modern medicine, science and technology always growing. There must be even better ways to deal with criminals now too.

Wrong! As I sit here on Death Row after six years I can think of many ways to make me proud to be an American. But I am not proud, nor do I agree with the way that we as Americans claim to be 'handling' our crime problems. From my perspective, things have not changed from the days when life was not considered valuable. We have not lessened the amount of crime nor have we killed it. I believe that no matter how many people we kill, the reasons for crime will go untreated.

Being on Death Row people learn to live their lives in the harshest ways. For years and years you wait until your case is finally decided in the courts. While I wait for my decision I sit daily and watch the harassment, torment, hate, anger, physical abuse, verbal abuse, loneliness, and even love at its utmost. I see people driven to the point of seeming insanity, or perhaps even truly being insane. I see people who lose themselves inside.

Death Row is a creation of Hell. Not only because you wear a burden on your back knowing your life could be forfeited at any time; but also just dealing with the reality of day to day life on the Row.

When a man first comes to Death Row the first thing he experiences is the loneliness. You are locked up in a five foot by eight foot cell all of your own. It comes complete with a toilet, a sink, and a bunk that is always too short for you. No one really knows what loneliness is until they come to the Row. No matter how many letters you get or write; no matter how many friends you make; from day one there is a big compartment in your heart that is labelled loneliness. On the Row a person feels lost in deep despair.

You feel no one will ever be able to help you. All is lost.

Most men are like me. I try to make myself believe in a better day. I try to live on dreams that I know may never come. I try to fool myself into making each new day a day closer to that dream. But as each day comes, the keepers and tormentors come alive with the sun. They send me back into reality.

Thirty men have been executed in Huntsville, Texas where I live. I personally knew most of the men. They were men who dreamed of a better life, a new way. Their miracle never came.

When these men were executed by my country I cried when I was by myself in the wee hours of the mornings. I cried because they were my friends. I cried because I knew the hell their families had been going through. I cried because I knew the hell they'd been through and that now it was over and they were in a better place. I cried for all our failures... mine, yours, theirs, everyone's. I cried because I know that two wrongs will never make a right.

As I sit in my cell right now, my neighbour in the next cell over is hollering, 'I rebuke you Satan, in the name of Jesus,' over and over again, loud enough for everyone on the block to hear. Most of the time he's mentally unstable. He fears for his life to the point of trusting no one. He won't eat most of the time because he believes the guards are trying to poison him. He goes on recreation by himself because he is afraid that the State will set him up and have him killed. Sometimes, when he's his real self, he's a pretty nice guy. But the guards constantly harass him to set him off. They have turned his water off for days. I've had to pass him water to drink. When the stink gets bad enough they turn on the water so he can flush his toilet.

There are almost 300 men here on Death Row in Texas. The numbers grow higher every day. Most men will have to develop a strong will to survive from the beginning to keep from falling into the frame of mind of the man that I just spoke about. Not all of us are like this man; some are worse and some are not. But I think that all of us do become infected in some way with this disease of the mind.

Why does it happen? Imagine that you are in a five by eight foot cell, seven days a week. You are only let out to shower and have recreation time for 15 hours per week. You may also have a visit once a week, if you are one of the very lucky ones who gets visits. The rest of the time you sit or lay and watch the bars that are covered in a heavy wire mesh which you can barely see through. You write letters, you read, or you might work on small craft projects if you can concentrate long enough, and provided you are able to afford this luxury. Each day you watch the news, read papers, and wait for the mail to come, hoping that someone will say the nightmare is over. But when night comes you are again wondering if it will ever be over and you pray for a better day tomorrow.

Many men develop close friendships on the Row. Friendships that can only be formed under extreme duress. You see a side to men on the Row that you would never see if they were free. Here they are free of drugs and alcohol. Most of them have found God and are deeply involved in religion. They realize God has forgiven them. They grieve and wonder why society cannot.

But no matter if you are insane or not; or in religion or somewhere in between or beyond, you are harassed day in and day out by our keepers. They not only destroy what little you have while searching through your cell, but they try to destroy what little faith you have left in humanity.

They are always right and you are always wrong. They are always perfect and you never were nor can you be. You are strip-searched every time you come or go. Stripped to the point where both men and women guards want to see up the crack of your ass and under your balls. Privacy does not exist here.

In this day and age I know that most people will respond by saying that we deserve what we get. That's what prison should be about. My response to that is that most men here committed their crime while on drugs, alcohol, or in an altered frame of mind. Our keepers are supposed to be role models and they specialize in humiliation and dehumanization. You don't rehabilitate people by killing them or by making them live a life of dehumanizing harassment to the point where they just don't care anymore.

I am surviving. I have not lost myself inside. I will pray again for a brighter day tomorrow.

Endeavor, August/September 1989

Plop, Plop, Fizz, Fizz

Phil Reeves and David Usborne

For days beforehand, the local radio stations ran trailers for their coverage of California's first execution in 25 years. Over the background of a tolling bell, or in one case of a snatch from Queen's 'Bohemian Rhapsody' ('Goodbye, everybody, I have got to go'), they promised the fastest, the fullest and the most lurid eyewitness accounts of Robert Alton Harris' last moments in the gas chamber.

The day before the execution, a van toured the streets around San Quentin prison bearing the twin slogans: 'Proud to be American' and 'Suck the Pipe, Bobbie!'. Demonstrators borrowed an old Alka-Seltzer advertising line for their placards: 'Plop, Plop, Fizz, Fizz. Oh, what a relief it is' – the gas which killed Harris was created by dropping cyanide pills into acid.

When Harris entered the gas chamber for the second and final time, after the last desperate legal attempts to save him had failed, he is said to have appeared puzzled by the collection of people, mostly strangers, assembled to watch him die. There were 48 of them, including 18 journalists who emerged immediately afterwards to supply precise and lengthy descriptions of his finals gasps in long interviews and press conferences carried live on television.

No public execution has been carried out in America since 1937, but this one came pretty close. And the one element that was missing – the pictures – may yet be supplied. Harris' gassing was videotaped on the orders of a US district judge, who believes the tape will help determine whether the gas chamber violates a clause in the US constitution forbidding cruel and unusual punishment. If and when it is introduced as evidence in a public court hearing, the footage may be released to the media. Several broadcasting companies have already expressed an interest in screening it.

No one would attempt to portray Robert Alton Harris as a pleasant man. When he brutally murdered his two young victims in 1978 he was on parole for manslaughter for beating a man to death. But the extent to which he was responsible for his actions will always be open to doubt. Refusing one last-minute plea for clemency, Pete Wilson, California's Republican governor, accepted that Harris was monstrously abused as a child. Nor did he dispute medical evidence produced by the defence that Harris suffered foetal alcohol syndrome – brain damage caused by his mother's drinking.

There was a hint of Harris' stunted development in the detail of his death. His last meal – a 21-piece tub of 'extra crispy' Kentucky Fried Chicken, Domino's pizzas, a six-pack of Pepsi, and a bag of jelly beans – was the kind of meal a child would order. As a final wish, he wanted everyone on San Quentin's Death Row to be treated to ice-cream. Even his last formal statement, (taken from a film called *Bill and Ted's Bogus Journey*) smacked of a bewildered juvenile: 'You can be a king or a street sweeper, but everybody dances with the grim reaper.'

But whether Harris was a culpable monster or a deranged victim of circumstance, whether his death was justice or revenge, does not alter one outstanding fact. The death penalty is winning in America, and the public likes it and wants more.

California, the fun state, the rich state, America's frontier with the future, is not back in the business of killing its killers. Michael Rushford, president of the Criminal Justice Legal Foundation, a law enforcement lobby group, commented: 'I'm not shouting with glee, but I think the gas chamber is going to be busy. This case has cleaned out the pipeline in the toughest legal battle zone in the country, California.'

Since 1992 began, three other states, Arizona, Delaware and Wyoming, have joined the execution club, raising its number to 20 states. Across the US, 13 people have been executed already this year, just one fewer than in the whole of 1991. In Texas, the state most devoted to the death penalty, where a quarter of all American executions are carried out, four men have been scheduled to die this month alone.

One of them, Billy White, a rubbish van driver aged 34, succumbed to his lethal injection in Huntsville prison two days after Harris. He had spent 14 years on Death Row; it took the medical attendants 40 minutes to find a vein for the needles, and it took him nine minutes to die. His passing, though by no means treated as an everyday matter, was attended by little of the popular frenzy seen in California. He was the 170th person to suffer the death penalty in the United States since the Supreme Court authorized the resumption of executions in 1976.

Why is this happening when across the globe the death penalty is in retreat? The new democracies of Eastern Europe are sweeping it away. Russia, until recently given to executing hundreds every year, is changing its habits. South Africa has declared a moratorium. As for the Western democracies with which the US normally compares itself, none are currently executing their citizens.

Although it was but one of 170 or but one of the 2,500 on Death Row in America, the case of Robert Alton Harris provides almost all the answers, writ large as everything is in California.

On the face of things, those who approved of Harris' execution had plenty of rhetorical ammunition. They could point to the three toddlers killed over the past 10 days in gang violence in Los Angeles, or the 60-odd people murdered so far this year in Oakland alone, or the 25,000 homicides across the country every year. People feel an intense desire to see violent crime contained. For most, that means employing the most extreme means. Opinion polls show a solid 75 per cent of the population in favour of the death penalty for premeditated murder.

This should not be taken as proof of a faith in deterrence. In the Californian debate, few people argued that Harris' death would prevent other deaths. The majority of American murders are committed by gang members who live daily with the prospect of being mown down by a rival's machine-gun. A death by gassing in a distant prison will not make the slightest difference to them.

One clue to the American view came in the final hours before Harris died, as an odd assortment of protesters gathered outside the gates of San Quentin prison, watched by a line of guards in riot helmets. Eventually, heated arguments erupted. Those in favour of Harris' death did not use the 'eye for an eye' argument alone, but their Old Testament banners spoke for them: 'The murderer shall surely be put to death' (*Numbers* 35, 16).

There was another clue inside the prison. Among the last faces Harris saw was one he knew. Steven Baker, the father of one of his victims, stood staring hard at him through the chamber's windows from a distance of six feet. For Mr Baker, it was the end of a 14-year campaign to see his son's killer die. He saw Harris mouth the words 'I'm sorry' as the gas began to choke him.

It was an important moment. Mr Baker saw his son's killer express remorse. But was it the moment for which the victims' relatives had been allowed in? This is Andy Mayeski, brother of the other of the two 16-year-old boys that Harris murdered: 'You still have the anger and you still have the pain. I mean you probably never lose that, for the love of your brother and his friend. But, beside that, I feel that the other family can now feel what it's like to lose a brother.'

A desire for punishment, and not a little revenge, is what moves Americans. They do not believe executions will stop crime, but they want a killer to get what they think he deserves.

Few indeed are the politicians willing to stand up against this. As Henry Schwarzchild, one of America's most prominent death penalty opponents, puts it: 'A lot of politicians have finked out on the issue. It is one thing to oppose it when 55 per cent of the public is against you on the issue, it is another to oppose it when 75 per cent of the public is against you.

One who paid the price was Governor Michael Dukakis, defeated by George Bush in 1988. His opposition to the death penalty was ruthlessly exploited by Mr Bush, who painted him in television ads as being soft on crime. And one who has learnt the lesson is Bill Clinton, the assumed Democratic challenger this time, who broke off from his campaign to supervise the execution in Arkansas of a man found guilty of murdering a police officer. The man had attempted to shoot himself after the incident and went to the electric chair severely brain damaged.

Death Row roll call

At the end of 1991 there were 2,547 prisoners on Death Row in 34 states.

Thirteen people have been executed in the United States already this year, compared with 14 in the whole of 1991.

David Gaskins, executed in South Carolina last year, was the first white man to suffer the death penalty for the murder of one black victim since 1944.

Since executions restarted in the US in 1977 170 people have been put to death.

At end 1991, 33 juvenile offenders were under sentence of death.

The eight longest-serving inmates of Death Row were all first sentenced to death in 1974.

A new sentence of death is passed in the US every day of the working week.

In 1987 a US District Court in Texas ruled that James Russell was 'not entitled to relief solely because [his lawyer] may have been intoxicated during the trial.' He was executed last September.

In 1989 the Supreme Court ruled that it was constitutional to execute both juveniles and the mentally ill.

Thirty-six states have the death penalty. Those which do not are Alaska, Hawaii, Iowa, Kansas, Maine, Massachusetts, Michigan, Minnesota, New York, North Dakota, Rhode Island, Vermont, West Virginia, Wisconsin.

One in four US executions takes place in Texas.

Last year, Governor Richard Celeste of Ohio marked his retirement by commuting eight death sentences. His successor immediately went to court to have the sentences restored.

Black defendants convicted of the murder of white victims are up to 11 times more likely than white defendants to receive the death penalty.

Jerry Bird, 52, was executed in Texas last year eight days after he suffered a stroke.

In 1991 there were 25,000 homicides in the US, an increase of 1,560 over 1990.

Willie Darden, executed in Florida in 1988, had survived six death warrants on last-minute appeals.

In New York State only the refusal of Governor Mario Cuomo to sign bills passed by the state legislature has prevented the reintroduction of the death penalty.

California was the fourth state this year to end a long spell without executions. The others are Arizona, Delaware and Wyoming.

Johnny Garrett was executed in Texas on 11 February for a murder he committed at the age of 17. An appeal for clemency from the Pope was rejected.

The execution of people whose crimes were committed when they were under 18 is banned under the United Nation's International Convention on Civil and Political Rights. The US has signed, but never ratified it.

Researchers studing murders in New York state in 1907-63 found that on average there were two additional murders in the month after an execution.

Independent on Sunday,
26 April 1992

Welcome to Hell: Part 1

Toby Williams

In this letter Toby Williams, convicted of murder in 1985 at the age of 21, describes how he feels after five years on Death Row in Huntsville, Texas.

As I look out the window into the free world (a window we call a television set), I often hear many misguided voices speaking out about people being convicted of murder who should never be released no matter what, because it is impossible to rehabilitate a person after they've committed murder. Firstly, how do you rehabilitate 'heat of the moment'?

We're portrayed as animals by many who know nothing about us or our cases, primarily for just being in this position, guilty or not. But since it is possible for an animal to be tamed and trained, we may as well be portrayed as less than an animal since it is impossible to be rehabilitated.

Although I've been enduring this pain for over five years (since 27.9.85 on Death Row), I've learned a lot and I've found new interests such as calligraphy, poetry, writing, collecting stamps, art string, art, and building such crafts as jewellery boxes, crosses and picture frames. And although I'm in this misfortunate position I still have feelings, a heart, I still know how to care, and help others, and most of all, I still know how to love. With the help of God – who I strongly believe in – I'm able to pull up a smile even in my most depressing moments.

Since I'm stripped of so much, I often wonder how long before I'm stripped of even those things God has allowed me to maintain.

1990

Welcome to Hell: Part 2

Vic Roberts

Vic Roberts, on Death Row in a prison in Georgia, describes his feelings of isolation.

Think constantly of us, as if chained with us.

Death Row is not just fences, bars and steel doors, bad guys and bad food. No, Death Row can be and should be compared with existing not living. It is filled with people with isolated hearts and suppressed minds; with loneliness that leaves one with an internal and external need for love and affection – and ideas, desires and feelings that we should be doing something constructive and positive. But the dreary anxiety pushes and swells, uncertainty smothers, suffocates, until it finally absorbs the imagination. Death Row is agonizing frustration, fruitless despair and unfamiliar indifference.

I am on Death Row. Why does my heart ache? Why will correspondence, caring, love and affection give much needed pleasure and satisfaction? All around me is suppressed and dead. It crushes in on me. Even the walls of my conscience seem to close in on me. It makes me inelastic. It is life without meaning, life without purpose. It is, indeed, no life at all.

I can easily stand criticism, correction, incarceration, even punishment. But the silence, the isolation, the unforgivingness from society – even from the churches, the pastors, the Christians – is terrifying and debilitating. Does anyone care? Does anyone care to know who I am or to know of the love I hold within my being?

Death Row is a place where many of us struggle to find answers in our own debilitating, enfeebled self, because there is no one to listen or to try to understand. It is a place of endless routines, where Time itself is a dreadful task. It is the Pit of

Hopelessness. But the most heartbreaking thing about Death Row is watching as society goes to church, kneels before the 'Father' and asks Him to bless their lives with peace, happiness and joy, watching as society pays its tithes, but seeing that they are still very much in debt because their debt lies unpaid for years, lurking in their souls.

It is not the freezing winter cold nor the heat and humidity of summer that depresses and spiritually disrupts, but the waiting in anxious anticipation for the letter, the card that never arrives; the waiting in pure faith for the visit from a loved one who never comes. No one comes because no one cares.

1990

Media Issues

An Enemy of the People

Arthur Miller

Dr Stockmann has discovered that the town springs – which attract an important and profitable tourist trade to Kirsten Springs – are poisonous. He takes his story to the local newspaper which is initially delighted to carry such a scoop. But when Stockmann's brother Peter, the town mayor, arrives he points out that if the springs are closed for repair the tourist trade will be lost and taxes will have to rise. Should the newspaper now carry a story which could destroy the town's future?

Characters

Billing	*Newspaper employee*
Hovstad	*Fiery and rebellious newspaper editor*
Dr Stockmann	*Writer of the article exposing the dangers of the town springs*
Aslaksen	*Printer*
Peter Stockmann	*Dr Stockmann's brother and town mayor*

(The editorial office of the People's Daily Messenger. *At the back of the room, to the left, is a door leading to the printing room. Near it, in the left wall, is another door. At the right of the stage is the entrance door. In the middle of the room there is a large table covered with papers, newspapers, and books. Around it are a few chairs. A writing desk stands against the right wall. The room is dingy and cheerless, the furniture shabby.*

As the curtain rises, Billing is sitting at the desk, reading the manuscripts. Hovstad comes in after a moment from the printing room. Billing looks up.)

Billing: The Doctor not come yet?
Hovstad: No, not yet. You finish it?

Billing holds up a hand to signal 'just a moment'. He reads on, the last paragraph of the manuscript. Hovstad comes and stands over him, reading with him. Now Billing closes the manuscript, glances up at Hovstad with some trepidation, then looks off. Hovstad, looking at Billing, walks a few steps away.

Hovstad: Well? What do you think of it?

Billing: *(with some hesitation)* It's devastating. The Doctor is a brilliant man. I swear, I myself never really understood how incompetent those fat fellows are, on top. *(He picks up the manuscript and waves it a little.)* I hear the rumble of revolution in this.

Hovstad: *(Looking toward the door)* Sssh! Aslaksen's inside.

Billing: Aslaksen's a coward. With all that moderation talk, all he's saying is, he's yellow. You're going to print this, aren't you?

Hovstad: Sure, I'm just waiting for the Doctor to give the word. If his brother hasn't given in, we put it on the press anyway.

Billing: Yes, but if the Mayor's against this it's going to get pretty rough. You know that, don't you?

Hovstad: Just let him try to block the reconstruction – the little businessmen and the whole town'll be screaming for his head. Aslaksen'll see to that.

Billing: *(Ecstatically)* The stockholders'll have to lay out a fortune of money if this goes through!

Hovstad: My boy, I think it's going to bust them. And when the springs go busted, the people are finally going to understand the level of genius that's been running this town. Those five sheets of paper are going to put in a liberal administration once and for all.

Billing: It's a revolution. You know that? *(With hope and fear)* I mean it, we're on the edge of a real revolution!

Dr Stockmann: *(Entering)* Put it on the press!

Hovstad: *(Excited)* Wonderful! What did the Mayor say?

Dr Stockmann: The Mayor has declared war, so war is what it's going to be *(He takes the manuscript from Billing.)* And this is only the beginning! You know what he tried to do?

Billing: *(Calling into the printing room)* Mr Aslaksen, the Doctor's here!

Dr Stockmann: *(Continuing)* He actually tried to blackmail me! He'd got the nerve to tell me that I'm not allowed to speak my mind without his permission! Imagine the shameless effrontery!

Hovstad: He actually said it right out?

Dr Stockmann: Right to my face! The trouble with me was I kept giving them credit for being our kind of people, but they're dictators! They're people who'll try to hold power even if they have to poison the town to do it.

(Towards the last part of Dr Stockmann's speech Aslaksen enters.)

Aslaksen: Now take it easy, Doctor, you – you mustn't always be throwing accusations. I'm with you, you understand, but moderation –

Dr Stockmann: *(Cutting him off)* What'd you think of the article, Hovstad?

Hovstad: It's a masterpiece. In one blow you've managed to prove beyond any doubt what kind of men are running us.

Aslaksen: May we print it now, then?

Dr Stockmann: I should say *so*!

Hovstad: We'll have it ready for tomorrow's paper.

Dr Stockmann: And listen, Mr Aslaksen, do me a favour, will you? You run a fine paper, but supervise the printing personally, eh? I'd hate to see the weather report stuck into the middle of my article.

Aslaksen: *(Laughing)* Don't worry, that won't happen this time!

Dr Stockmann: Make it perfect, eh? Like you were printing money. You can't imagine how I'm dying to see it in print. After all the lies in the papers, the half-lies, the quarter-lies – to finally see the absolute, unvarnished truth about something important. And this is only the beginning. We'll go on to other subjects and blow up every lie we live by! What do you say, Aslaksen?

Aslaksen: *(Nodding in agreement)* But just remember...

Billing and Hovstad together with Aslaksen: Moderation!

Aslaksen: *(To Billing and Hovstad)* I don't know what's so funny about that!

Billing: *(Enthralled)* Doctor Stockmann, I feel as though I were standing in some historic painting. Goddammit, this is a historic day! Someday this scene'll be in a museum, entitled, 'The Day the Truth Was Born'...

Peter Stockman: *(Entering)* Thank you.

(Hovstad carefully closes the door.)

Peter Stockmann: *(Walking around)* It's clean! I always imagined this place would look dirty. But it's clean. *(Commendingly)* Very nice, Mr Aslaksen. *(He puts his hat on the desk.)*

Aslaksen: Not at all, Your Honour – I mean to say, I always...

Hovstad: What can I do for you, Your Honour? Sit down?

Peter Stockmann: *(Sits, placing his can on the table)* I had a very annoying thing happen today, Mr Hovstad.

Hovstad: That so?

Peter Stockmann: It seems my brother has written some sort of – memorandum. About the springs.

Hovstad: You don't say.

Peter Stockmann: *(Looking at Hovstad now)* He mentioned it... to you?

Hovstad: Yes. I think he said something about it.

Aslaksen: *(Nervously starts to go out, attempting to hide the manuscript)* Will you excuse me, gentlemen...

Peter Stockmann: *(Pointing to the manuscript)* That's it, isn't it?

Aslaksen: This? I don't know, I haven't had a chance to look at it, the printer just handed it to me...

Hovstad: Isn't that the thing the printer wanted the spelling checked?

Aslaksen: That's it. It's only a question of spelling. I'll be right back.

Peter Stockmann: I'm very good at spelling. *(He holds out his hand.)* Maybe I can help you.

Hovstad: No, Your Honour, there's some Latin in it. You wouldn't know Latin, would you?

Peter Stockmann: Oh, yes. I used to help my brother with his Latin all the time. Let me have it.

(Aslaksen gives him the manuscript. Peter Stockmann looks at the title on the first page, then glances up sarcastically at Hovstad who avoids his eyes.)

Peter Stockmann: You're going to print this?

Hovstad: I can't very well refuse a signed article. A signed article is the author's responsibility.

Peter Stockmann: Mr Aslaksen, you're going to allow this?

Aslaksen: I'm the publisher, not the editor, Your Honour. My policy is freedom for the editor.

Peter Stockmann: You have a point – I can see that.

Aslaksen: *(Reaching for the manuscript)* So if you don't mind...

Peter Stockmann: Not at all. *(But he holds on to the manuscript. After a pause)* This reconstruction of the springs –

Aslaksen: I realize, Your Honour – it does mean tremendous sacrifices for the stockholders.

Peter Stockmann: Don't upset yourself. The first thing a mayor learns is that the less wealthy can always be prevailed upon to demand a spirit of sacrifice for the public good.

Aslaksen: I'm glad you see that.

Peter Stockmann: Oh, yes. Especially when it's the wealthy who are going to do the sacrificing. What you don't seem to understand, Mr Aslaksen, is that so long as I am Mayor, any changes in those springs are going to be paid for by a municipal loan.

Aslaksen: A municipal – you mean you're going to tax the people for this?

Peter Stockmann: Exactly.

Hovstad: But the springs are a private corporation!

Peter Stockmann: The corporation built Kirsten Springs out of its own money. If the people want them changed, the people naturally must pay the bill. The corporation is in no position to put out any more money. It simply can't do it.

Aslaksen: *(To Hovstad)* That's impossible! People will never stand for a new tax. *(To the Mayor)* Is this a fact or your opinion?

Peter Stockmann: It happens to be a fact. Plus another fact – you'll forgive me for talking about facts in a newspaper office – but don't forget that the springs will take two years to make over. Two years without income for your small businessmen, Mr Aslaksen, and a heavy new tax besides. And all because *(His private emotion comes to the surface; he throttles* the manuscript in his hand.) – because of this dream, this hallucination, that we live in a pesthole!

Hovstad: That's based on science.

Peter Stockmann: *(Raising the manuscript and throwing it down on the table)* This is based on vindictiveness, on his hatred of authority and nothing else. *(He pounds on the manuscript.)* This is the mad dream of a man who is trying to blow up our way of life! It has nothing to do with reform or science or anything else, but pure and simple destruction! And I intend to see to it that the people understand it exactly so!

Aslaksen: *(Hit by this)* My God! *(To Hovstad)* Maybe... You sure you want to support this thing, Hovstad?

Hovstad: *(Nervously)* Frankly I'd never thought of it in quite that way. I mean... *(To the Mayor)* When you think of it psychologically it's completely possible, of course, that the man is simply out to – I don't know what to say, Your Honour. I'd hate to hurt the town in any way. I never imagined we'd have to have a new tax.

Peter Stockmann: You should have imagined it because you're going to have to advocate it. Unless, of course, liberal and radical newspaper readers enjoy high taxes. But you'd know that better than I. I happen to have here a brief story of the actual facts. It proves that, with a little care, nobody need be harmed at all by the water.

(from Act 2 Scene 1)

Is That It?

Bob Geldof

It was coming to the end of 1984 and I could see no prospect for the release of an album the Boomtown Rats and I had sweated over and were proud of. All day I had been on the phone trying to promote a single from the album. I went home in a state of blank resignation and switched on the television. But there I saw something that placed my worries in a ghastly new perspective.

The news report was of famine in Ethiopia. From the first seconds it was clear that this was a horror on a monumental scale. The pictures were of people who were so shrunken by starvation that they looked like beings from another planet. Their arms and legs were as thin as sticks, their bodies spindly. Swollen veins and huge, blankly staring eyes protruded from their shrivelled heads. The camera wandered amid them like a mesmerized observer, occasionally dwelling on one person so that he looked directly at me, sitting in my comfortable living-room. And there were children, their bodies fragile and vulnerable as premature babies but with the consciousness of what is happening to them gleaming dully from their eyes. All around was the murmur of death like hoarse whisper, or the buzzing of flies.

From the first few seconds it was clear that this was a tragedy which the world had somehow contrived not to notice until it had reached a scale which constituted an international scandal. You could hear that in the tones of BBC reporter Michael Buerk. It was the voice of a man who was registering despair, grief and disgust at what he was seeing. At the end the newscaster remained silent. Paula burst into tears, and then rushed upstairs to check on our baby, Fifi, who was sleeping peacefully in her cot.

The images played and replayed in my mind. What could I do? Did not the sheer scale of the thing call for something more?

Michael Buerk had used the word biblical: a famine of biblical proportions. A horror like this could not occur today without our consent. We had allowed this to happen. I would send money. But that was not enough. I was stood against the wall. I had to withdraw my consent. What else could I do? I was only a pop singer – and by now not a very successful pop singer. All I could do was make records that no one bought. But I would do that, I would give the profits of the next Rats record to Oxfam. What good would that do? It would be a pitiful amount. But it would be more than I could raise by simply dipping into my shrunken bank account. Maybe some people would buy it just because the profits were going to Oxfam. And I would withdraw my consent. Yet that was not enough.

1986

The Challenger Disaster

Peggy Noonan

In 1986, a US space shuttle, Challenger, exploded shortly after take-off, an event witnessed by TV viewers all around the world. President Ronald Reagan was due to make a formal address to the American people that evening. Peggy Noonan, his speech writer, wrote this in its place.

'Ladies and gentlemen, I had planned to speak to you tonight to report on the State of the Union, but the events of earlier today have led me to change those plans. Today is a day for mourning and remembering.

'We know we share this pain with all of the people of our country. This is truly a national loss.

'Nineteen years ago almost to the day, we lost three astronauts in a terrible accident on the ground. But we have never lost an astronaut in flight. We have never had a tragedy like this. And perhaps we have forgotten the courage it took for the crew of the shuttle. But they, the *Challenger* Seven, were aware of the dangers – and overcame them, and did their jobs brilliantly.

'We mourn seven heroes – Michael Smith, Dick Scobee, Judith Resnik, Ronald McNair, Ellison Onizuka, Gregory Jarvis, and Christa McAuliffe. We mourn their loss as a nation, together.

'To the families of the Seven: we cannot bear, as you do, the full impact of this tragedy – but we feel the loss, and we are thinking about you so very much. Your loved ones were daring and brave and they had that special grace, that special spirit that says, "Give me a challenge and I'll meet it with joy." They had a hunger to explore the universe and discover its truths. They wished to serve and they did – they served us all.

'And I want to say something to the schoolchildren of America who were watching the live coverage of the shuttle's take-off.

I know it's hard to understand, but sometimes painful things like this happen – it's all part of the process of exploration and discovery – it's all part of taking a chance and expanding man's horizons. The future doesn't belong to the fainthearted, it belongs to the brave. The *Challenger* crew was pulling us into the future – and we'll continue to follow them.

'I've always had great faith in and respect for our space programme – and what happened today does nothing to diminish it. We don't hide our space programme, we don't keep secrets and cover things up, we do it all up front and in public. That's the way freedom is, and we wouldn't change it for a minute.

'We'll continue our quest in space. There will be more shuttle flights and more shuttle crews and, yes, more volunteers, more civilians, more teachers in space. Nothing ends here – our hopes and our journeys continue.

'I want to add that I wish I could talk to every man and woman who works for NASA or who worked on this mission and tell them: "Your dedication and professionalism have moved and impressed us for decades, and we know of your anguish. We share it."

'There's a coincidence today. On this day 390 years ago the great explorer Sir Francis Drake died aboard ship off the coast of Panama. In his lifetime the great frontiers were the oceans, and a historian later said, "He lived by the sea, died on it, and was buried in it." Today we can say of the *Challenger* Crew: their dedication was, like Drake's, complete.

'The crew of the space shuttle *Challenger* honoured us by the manner in which they lived their lives. We will never forget them, nor the last time we saw them – this morning, as they prepared for their journey, and waved goodbye, and "slipped the surly bonds of earth" to "touch the face of God." '

1986

Up and Down the City Road

The Weasel

I have a letter from Mrs A Booker in Weymouth expressing 'distress and nausea' at having to see a photograph of a dead child in an 'otherwise excellent' feature about the situation in Bosnia which was published in this magazine two weeks ago. 'I do not need to see what a slaughtered infant looks like; I can imagine it only too well, looking at my own sleeping children', writes Mrs Booker. 'It may be an unfashionable platitude, but human life *is* sacred. Showing its desecration is neither arty nor clever, but simply sickening.'

I sympathize most strongly with Mrs Booker's point of view, for only the depraved could possibly enjoy looking at a picture of a murdered child. Is she therefore justified in censuring us for publishing it? Many readers will doubtless think she is, but I am not so sure. It is a very difficult question to which, it seems to me, there is no straightforward answer.

The purpose of many recent reports from Bosnia has been to impress upon a largely skeptical and apathetic British public the horror and tragedy of what is happening there, with a view to creating political pressure for some kind of intervention by western governments. Assuming this purpose to be a good one, how is it best to be achieved? Is it enough to write forcefully about what is going on, or will most readers remain unmoved unless the horror is conveyed to them in pictures?

The answer to the last question, unfortunately, seems to be yes. In every great human tragedy of recent times, it always seems to have been pictures that have pricked people's consciences and provoked them to demand political action. Would the Americans have turned against the Vietnam War if they had not been surfeited with sickening images on television? Would Bob Geldof ever have raised such huge sums for famine relief in Africa if the BBC had not filled our television screens with heartbreaking pictures of starving children? Two years ago in this magazine we published some distressing photographs of Cambodians who had lost limbs in accidents with mines laid by the Khmer Rouge. Our readers immediately donated £60,000 to the Cambodia Trust, a British charity founded to help victims of the Cambodian civil war. Would they have done so otherwise? Clearly not.

There seems, then, to be little doubt that pictures can be exremely effective in ramming home a political message that might otherwise fall on deaf ears. But this does not make it any easier to decide what sort of pictures to use – or not to use – in any given context. Too much horror can repel rather than warm the heart. Certain kinds of pictures – of children with swollen bellies and twig-like limbs, for example – can become excessively familiar and therefore merely depressing in their effect.

Finally, there is Mrs Booker's revulsion at the idea that 'artiness' should play a part in the selection and presentation of photographs of human tragedy. The picture of the dead boy to which she took such strong exception was, in fact, a beautiful photograph, and I would find it very understandable if it was in part its beauty that repelled her. It is very unfair, but it can only too easily seem like heartlessness and exploitation on the photographer's part to take too beautiful a picture of a dead child. On the other hand, the more beautiful the picture, the greater the dignity the child seems to acquire, and the greater the sympathy the reader is likely to feel.

Independent Magazine, 15 August 1992

Page 3 Letters

Dear Sir or mrs,
I wrote to the Sun and this is a copy of the letter that he sent to me. That's what he thinks.
I think he's rather mean because we get sick of it
All the boys pick on the ladies and make fun of them and everyone laughs at them. why would they want to put something like that in?
why don't they put men in?
why do the women let them do it?
I think the women who do it are silly Because they shouldn't show other people what they've got. Could you please tell the other newspapers to stop putting the pictures in because i get sick of it.
Alot of children at our School bring the Sun newspaper in for painting and the boys look at them in stead of using them for painting.
We had a vote on whether more people wanted to stop putting these photographs in the paper, or carry on and this was the result.

STOP		CARRY ON	
Boys	5	Boys	9
girls	15	girls	3
Alltogether	20	Alltogether	12

from
Zoë (Age 8)
and
Sharron (Age 8)

Registered Office

News Group Newspapers Ltd.
A Subsidiary of News International Ltd.

30 Bouverie Street, Fleet Street, London, EC4Y 8DE.

Registered No. 679215 England
Telex: Sunnews 267827
Telephone 01-353 3030

8th October 1980

Dear Zoe

Thank you for your letter.

We can only say to you what we said to another young lady from your school, Sharon Randell. That is, inspite of what you may have been told, there is nothing "rude" about our pictures of unclothed ladies and on occasion men as in the Daily Male feature. The Model girls who pose for the pictures are not being made fun of at all. They are greatly respected for their beauty and every year we get hundreds of letters from girls whose ambition is to have their picture on Page 3 of The Sun.

If we stopped putting these pictures in the paper many of our readers would write and complain - and not all would be from male readers.

Thanks again for your interest in The Sun.

Best wishes

Yours sincerely

Paul Buttle
Picture Editor

THE PRESS COUNCIL

No. 1 SALISBURY SQUARE, LONDON EC4Y 8AE

ESTABLISHED 1953
Tel: 01-353 1248

Chairman: F. P. NEILL Q.C.
Director: KENNETH MORGAN O.B.E.

Please quote our reference: R8098

FIRST CLASS
24 Nov 80

Dear Zoe and Sharon,

Thank you very much for your letter about the pictures in THE SUN and for sending me a copy of the letter which the picture editor of THE SUN sent to you.

I was very interested in your letter and especially that you and the others in your class went to the trouble of having a vote about whether you wanted pictures like these to go on being published in newspapers.

I think it might be helpful if I told you a bit about the Press Council. It is a group of about 36 men and women. Half of them are people who work for newspapers and the other half are people from all kinds of jobs not connected with newspapers. They include housewives, teachers, a bishop, an admiral, trade union members, and people who do different jobs in offices. Together, under a chairman who is a lawyer, they consider complaints about what is printed in newspapers. The Press Council will tell the editor of a newspaper if it thinks something in his newspaper was unfair or untrue or wrong for some reason.

It cannot stop an editor from publishing in his newspaper the things which he thinks should be published and the things he thinks readers will want to see. It is important that neither the Press Council nor anyone else should be able to tell an editor what he must or most not put in his paper, because it is important that newspapers should be free.

Most people think that one of the good things about living in England is that there are lots of different newspapers and most readers can find one they like.

Although you and most of the girls in your class may not like the pictures of women which you see in THE SUN - and other newspapers - many people do like them because many people buy those newspapers.

THE PRESS
COUNCIL

page - 2 -

There are newspapers which do not have pictures of the kind you object to in them and perhaps when you begin buying newspapers yourselves you will choose that sort of newspaper. I think it is a good idea to let people choose for themselves even if they choose newspapers with things in them that you and most of the girls and some of the boys do not like.

As long as what appears in a newspaper is not untrue, or unfair to someone, and does not harm people, it is better that the newspaper should be free to print it than that anyone should have the power to stop it doing so.

I am sending you with this letter a leaflet which tells you a little more about the Press Council.

If I were you I would try to get some plain paper - or newspapers without many pictures in - for painting lessons!

Yours sincerely,

Kenneth Morgan.

KM/DH

Director

Enc: Leaflet 109.

Hillsborough

Peter Chippendale and Chris Horrie

In April 1989 a disaster caused by overcrowding at the Hillsborough Stadium led to the deaths of 95 Liverpool football supporters. Lord Justice Taylor was asked to lead the inquiry.

The Hillsborough tragedy, as Taylor bluntly concluded, was primarily the fault of the South Yorkshire police in charge of crowd control, with particular blame pinned in his report on the senior officer at the ground, Superintendent David Duckenfield. Games like these semi-finals, held on neutral territory, were always particularly nerve-racking for the authorities as the fans of both sides were off their familiar home ground and in this case, as the match moved towards its 3.00 p.m. start, a potentially lethal crush had developed outside the stadium with 5,000 Liverpool fans struggling to get through the bottleneck of the turnstiles.

To relieve the increasingly lethal pressure Duckenfield had given the order for the gates to be thrown open. But instead of routing the surging fans on to empty terraces, he had allowed them to take the automatic route through a tunnel into one of the pens which was already overcrowded, and from which there was no escape due to the wire cages enclosing the front. As the inevitable push forward began Duckenfield had then frozen in his control box and further compounded his error by treating the fans' desperate attempts to escape by scaling the cage as a pitch invasion. Only when it was too late had he allowed the emergency gates to be opened and the pressure relieved.

Few tragedies had been so comprehensively recorded. Every second of the drawn-out horror had unravelled itself, live, in front of a TV audience expecting an exciting afternoon's sports viewing. The mass of sports photographers had taken thousands of pictures, many of which showed such harrowing detail of death and suffering it was an almost impossible editorial decision to decide which could actually be printed.

With such searing and powerful material it was obvious straightaway that all the papers would be treading an impossible tightrope with their readers. Somehow they had to strike a balance between adequately portraying the full nightmare of being trapped, yet not use pictures showing such grotesque detail that their readers would be sickened. Seasoned veterans of the Street knew instantly that, short of printing no pictures at all, they could not win.

With the fierce competition between them, that decision was anyway out of the question. Any paper taking it would not only be ducking its responsibility to cover the news, but hoisting itself on the petard of the fundamental hypocrisy of the general public. Some people would bay for the blood of the papers printing the most horrific pictures, while at the same time others would pile into the shops to buy the ones with the most shocking images. Words, however, were a different matter and MacKenzie's [Editor of *The Sun*] personal achievement was to use them to turn Hillsborough into an unparalleled journalistic disaster, with huge and continuing financial consequences for his paper.

The story was first the province of the Sundays, for whom it was the biggest since Zeebrugge two years previously. Unprepared, and strapped by earlier edition times than the dailies, they could do little more than react blindly with scant opportunity for any effective analysis. False information disseminated by Superintendent Duckenfield who lied that the fans had stormed the gates and forced them to be opened, only complicated matters by jumbling up the first impressions.

By the time the Sundays were on the presses the full story was still in its early stages. Dazed parents and relatives, many of whom had just arrived from Liverpool, were still stumbling round Sheffield, inspecting the Polaroid pictures of the dead at the makeshift morgue in a gym next to the stadium, then scouring the city's hospitals in their desperate search for children and loved ones they only knew were missing, and could be safe, mangled or dead.

As the survivors made their way home the city of Liverpool closed ranks in stunned shock and disbelief. The local Liverpool *Echo* had crammed the first garbled reports into its late sports edition and now staff on their day off came into the office unprompted and went to their desks. Some, although they did not yet know it, had lost friends or relatives in the disaster. Vin Kelly, the associate editor running the paper while editor Chris Oakley was on holiday, took a snap decision to produce a special 28-page issue for sale on Sunday morning. As they started work Alf Green, the news editor, watched both reporters and subs vainly struggling to hold back their emotions as they pieced all the terrible individual stories together. For the first time in his 30-year career he saw men and women openly weeping as they worked and found themselves overwhelmed by the depth of the tragedy they were recording.

The *Echo*'s special edition went on the presses at 1 a.m., carrying on the front page a close-up picture of a man and a woman in the crush crying in distress and terror behind the wire of the cage. The headline read: OUR DAY OF TEARS. Alf Green thought the page, designed by deputy editor Joe Holmes, the most difficult exercise in taste the paper had ever faced. The picture was horrific, but the *Echo* was correct in its judgement that it captured the agony of the moment without the brutal detail of other pictures which were about to cause a major uproar when they appeared in the nationals. The paper succeeded in running it without complaint, partly – in Green's view – simply because it was the local paper, but also because of the headline, which softened the image. He thought it was right. It was what people were thinking.

The next day, as the city struggled to pull itself together, there was the fresh horror of the invasion by a newspaper pack, mob-handed for its grisly task of prising pictures and tear-jerking stories from parents, relatives and friends of the dead. Not just British, but foreign reporters, photographers and camera crews flooded into both Sheffield and Liverpool. *The Sun* was estimated to have piled 18 reporters and photographers on to the story.

Shortly after the disaster wild rumours had swept round that photographers on the spot had used their feet to turn over bodies on the pitch so they could get better pictures. Now a spate of stories followed about reporters desperate for quotes posing as social workers and Salvation Army helpers, ringing up Helplines pretending to be relatives or government officials, or trying to get their foot in the door by masquerading as journalists from the local *Echo*. Most of the rumours featured reporters alleged to be from *The Sun*, and, although none could be substantiated, the paper was in no position to complain. Whether they were true or false, it was merely reaping the reward of its public image.

On Monday *The Sun* cleared page after page after page for different pictures and stories, pulled together under a tacky logo labelled: GATES OF HELL. The pattern of 'earthquake journalism' set by Larry Lamb had been copied by the rest of the tabloids and further intensified throughout the 1980s. On this occasion the correctness of Lamb's thinking was demonstrated by the Sundays selling an extra 500,000 copies between them, while on the Monday public desire for more detail still seemed insatiable. *The Sun*, like the other dailies, had more time to reflect on which pictures to use. But as the official death list had not been published there was still no way it could tell in most cases whether the individuals pictured being crushed or lying on the pitch were now alive or dead. Like most of its rivals, it printed them regardless.

It was not *The Sun*, but the *Mirror* with its use of colour, so making the pictures even more ghoulish, which brought the wrath of Liverpool down on its head on Monday morning. The *Mirror*, carrying 16 pages on the story, filled the front page with a grisly picture showing horrible detail of fans who appeared already dead or dying jumbled together on top of each other. The use of colour added to the horror by showing how the victim's faces had turned blue as the oxygen was squeezed from their lungs. In all it was reminiscent of Hieronymus Bosch's vision of hell.

The outpouring of anger at the front page focused in on the local media, and particularly the two local radio stations Radio Merseyside, run by the BBC, and the commercial Radio City. At Radio Merseyside DJ Billy Butler had scrapped his popular morning *Hold Your Plums* show – normally three hours of the cheerful Scouse humour – to concentrate solely on the disaster.

Butler took the *Mirror* to task for cashing in on the disaster by printing the pictures, and as calls agreeing with him jammed the lines, he and producer Wally Scott decided that the *Mirror* should be rung to be asked to defend itself on the air. The call was made by Roger Phillips, who ran the station's *Newsline* programme. The *Mirror* responded promptly by putting on a senior executive, who explained that the paper stood by its decision. He justified showing the full horror of the event as a way of helping to ensure that steps were taken so nothing like it could ever happen in the future, which was why the paper had spashed: NEVER AGAIN. Phillips, like Butler, still thought the pictures had been printed to sell the paper – as did most of the people ringing in. He asked the exec. if he would have used that front page picture if it had been of his own children. 'No,' the *Mirror* spokesman candidly replied. So why do it to strangers? Phillips demanded. The spokesman was silent. The outcry about pictures was not restricted to the *Mirror*, or to the city of Liverpool. At the Press Council the phone started ringing itself off the hook, and practically every paper found itself deluged by a flood of angry callers and complaining letters.

But during the day on Monday a new and more sinister factor began to surface in the story. From the start there had been an understandable knee-jerk reaction of blaming hooligans for the disaster, and it was the preconditioning which had largely accounted for Superintendent Duckenfield's automatic assumption that the unfolding tragedy was a pitch invasion. Even when most of the deaths had already occurred, television commentators had fallen into the same trap by excitedly screaming that fans were tearing down the hoardings. They were – but only to use as makeshift stretchers.

Close Encounters with the Truth

Henry Porter

In this account, Henry Porter shows how some tabloid newspapers, in this case *The News of the World*, have decided that if fictional stories sell newspapers they could go a stage further and use science fiction.

In June 1983, while the rest of us were absorbed by the General Election, the paper turned on to extra-terrestrial matters. Under the headline CLOSE ENCOUNTER AT THE SHAMROCK CAFE, Keith Beabey and Pippa Sibley revealed that three women had been kidnapped by a UFO after they had spent a pleasant evening together near Wolverhampton. It started like this:

> Strange red and white lights hovered overhead as three women drove home from their weekly night out.
>
> Mysteriously their car came to a halt outside the Shamrock Café on the A5 in Shropshire, though the driver had her foot hard down on the accelerator.
>
> Then the lights suddenly vanished and the trio rushed excitedly to a nearby police station, where they reported a close encounter with a UFO.
>
> But that was when they noticed something even stranger happening. The drive to the police station should have taken five minutes. Instead it took 25.
>
> Only now, with the help of hypnosis, under the strictest supervision, has an explanation been found for those 20 missing minutes. And it is amazing.
>
> Each of the women has independently told the same story that they did have a close encounter, far closer than they first imagined. For each says that she was taken aboard a spacecraft, examined by alien beings and then released.

The paper then reproduced the accounts of each of the three women, Rosemary Hawkins, Valerie Walters, and Viv Hayward. Here is Rosemary's:

> Bright lights. White tinged with yellow and red. So strange its three [sic]. No sound.
>
> We are frightened the lights are attached to a spacecraft of some kind.
>
> I am floating and I'm not in the car any more with Viv or Val, I feel big and bloated.
>
> It's a semicircular room. I'm on a bed in the room like a long table on a stand.
>
> There's something coming. I can hear them. Something is in the room. It's metal. It doesn't walk, it sort of rolls on wheels.
>
> It's about four feet tall, round on the top with a round body and round legs.
>
> It's looking at me. There's more coming. It's the same noise. There are four. They are around me.
>
> They haven't got a face. Their heads move up and down. That's how I know they are talking to me.
>
> They don't seem to be nasty. They just want to have a look. I feel so relaxed and friendly. I like them.

By contrast Viv found the aliens rather frightening. They put their hands inside her legs and pulled her bones about a bit and then released her. She described them thus: 'They are four feet tall. They have no hair. They are ugly. They have strange-looking noses; thin arms, I can't see their legs. They are dressed in green cloaks.'

This entertaining scoop was accompanied by an equally entertaining drawing of one of the women being examined by those curious little beings from another world, who anyone who used to read *Eagle* would recognize. As far as I remember your average Martian is always made of metal, favours the colour green, never has a face, is unfailingly inquisitive and is always lacking in stature. Tempting though it was to entertain the idea that a flying saucer had landed near the Shamrock Café on the A5, everyone chose to ignore *The News of the World*'s revelations.

Undaunted, in October the paper announced: UFO LANDS IN SUFFOLK – AND THAT'S OFFICIAL. Mr Keith Beabey it was, again, who wrote:

> A UFO has landed in Britain – and that staggering fact has been officially confirmed.
>
> Despite a massive cover-up *News of the World* investigators have proof that the mysterious craft came to earth in a red ball of light at 3 a.m. on December 27, 1980.
>
> It happened in a pine forest called Tangham Wood just half a mile from the United States Air Force base at RAF Woodbridge in Suffolk.
>
> An American airman who was there told us there were beings in silver space suits aboard the craft.
>
> Farm cattle and forest animals ran berserk as the spacecraft, a sloping silver dish about 20 feet across its base, silently glided to land in a blinding explosion of lights.
>
> About 200 military and civilian personnel, British and American, witnessed the event. The airman said the visitors appeared to be expected.

Can *The News of the World* believe that none of its readers have seen *Close Encounters of the Third Kind*? Obviously. The two main witnesses to the event are a man named 'Art Wallace', a junior airman whose identity is protected by *The News of the World* for 'security reasons' and Lt.-Colonel Charles Halt, deputy commander of the USAF 81st Tactical Fighter Wing stationed at Woodbridge. The latter filed a report to his superiors which went as follows:

> Early in the morning two USAF security police patrolmen saw unusual lights outside the back gate of Woodbridge.

Thinking an aircraft might have crashed or been forced down they called for permission to go outside the gate to investigate.

The on-duty flight chief allowed the three patrolmen to proceed on foot.

The individuals reported seeing a strange glowing object in the forest.

The object was described as being metallic in appearance and triangular in shape, approximately two to three metres across the base and approximately two metres high. It illuminated the entire forest with a white light.

The object had a pulsating red light on top and a bank of blue lights underneath. The object was hovering on legs. As the patrolmen approached the object it manoeuvred through the trees and disappeared.

At the time the animals on a nearby farm went into a frenzy. The object was sighted approximately an hour later near the back gate.

The next day three depressions one and a half inches deep and seven inches in diameter were found where the object had been sighted on the ground.

Later during the night a red sunlike light was seen through the trees. It moved about and pulsated. At one point it appeared to throw off glowing particles and then broke into five separate white objects and disappeared.

Immediately thereafter the red starlike objects were noted in the sky, two objects in the North and one in the South, all of which were about 10 degrees above the horizon. The objects moved rapidly and displayed green-blue lights. The objects in the North appeared elliptical through an 8–12 power lens.

They turned full circle. The objects in the North remained in the sky for an hour or more. The objects in the South were visible for two or three hours and beamed down a storm of lights from time to time.

Inside, the paper carried a startling interview with 'Art Wallace' who said that he had seen a craft with a green light on top and that he understood from his fellow patrolmen that there were little men inside wearing silver suits.

This time *The News of the World* was not entirely ignored. Adrian Berry, the level-headed Science Editor of *The Daily Telegraph*, wrote that he too had found a UFO and produced a picture of it hovering over St Paul's Cathedral in London. He wrote: 'Our photographer Paul Armiger was standing beside St Paul's when this huge spaceship came roaring over his head. He knew its occupant must have flown all the way from Alpha Centauri to kidnap the Dean...'

He went on to suggest that *The News of the World*'s 'evidence' was, if anything, less convincing. He continued:

> All that had happened was that a United States Air Force Colonel at RAF Woodbridge had seen an unexplained light in the surrounding woods. This could only have been the rotating beam of Orford Ness lighthouse. The only problem when one looks into these stories is that usually the town cannot be found on any map and never existed, and the scientists did not utter a word of what they are quoted as saying, their remarks having been invented by unscrupulous reporters... Would alien visitors really seek information about humanity from the dullest and least reliable of mankind? Would they really rush about in disc-shaped vehicles with abysmal aerodynamic qualities?

Derek Jameson wrote to *The Daily Telegraph* to defend his paper's exclusive story, drawing Berry's attention to the depression mentioned in the Colonel's report. Berry had an answer for this too, which he was kind enough to share with us through the Letters column of his own paper: 'Mr Thurkettle, a Forestry Commission official, who examined the site, has attibuted the depressions to rabbits. The local police say that they were probably made by an animal.'

Berry had used the word 'impudence' to describe *The News of the World*'s report; it is hard to disagree. Here was a newspaper claiming that there had been official verification when there had been none, and that 200 people had been expecting the landing when only one could be found to talk about it – and even he wanted to remain anonymous.

The following Sunday the paper returned to the subject by revealing that there had been a SINISTER PLOT TO HUSH UP THE TRUTH. A section was devoted to our friend 'Art Wallace', who, it turns out, had tried to re-enlist with the air force but had been rejected because there was no record of his first term of service. He is quoted as saying that he may have been drugged and brainwashed.

With the country crawling with little silver men and the skies crowded with unidentified craft *The News of the World*'s sister paper, *The Sun*, eventually decided to ask the question that must have been at the back of many minds: IS YOUR NEIGHBOUR FROM OUTER SPACE? With the help of a UFO investigator named Brad Steiger and a theoretical biologist, Dr Thomas Easton, they gave eight tell-tale tip-offs that can give an alien away...

But perhaps one is being unjust in ridiculing this particular range of fiction from the Bouverie Street dream factory. The UFO articles were all commissioned in the belief that they would amuse the readership, which to an extent they must have. The only mistake seems to be for journalists like Derek Jameson to state in public that they believe their own stories.

Photojournalism Selection

The Blitz: police and fire-fighters battle for control during another night of bombing. 1940–41

Facing page top
Fear and defiance: an uprising of Polish Jews in the Warsaw ghetto is brutally crushed by Hitler's troops. Miraculously, the six year-old boy was to survive. 1943

Facing page bottom
Coastal assault: Normandy beaches swarm with Canadian soldiers, as the Allied invasion of Europe, known as D-Day, begins. June 6 1944

Under attack: the frigate *HMS Antelope* is hit by an Argentinian missile during the Falklands War. 1982

Facing page top
A soldier's-eye view: The US army moves supplies, through a deforested no man's land in Vietnam. 1968

Facing page bottom
'One small step for man': Buzz Aldrin sets foot on the moon, the first human being on another planet. Fellow astronaut, Neil Armstrong, called it 'A giant step for mankind'. 1969

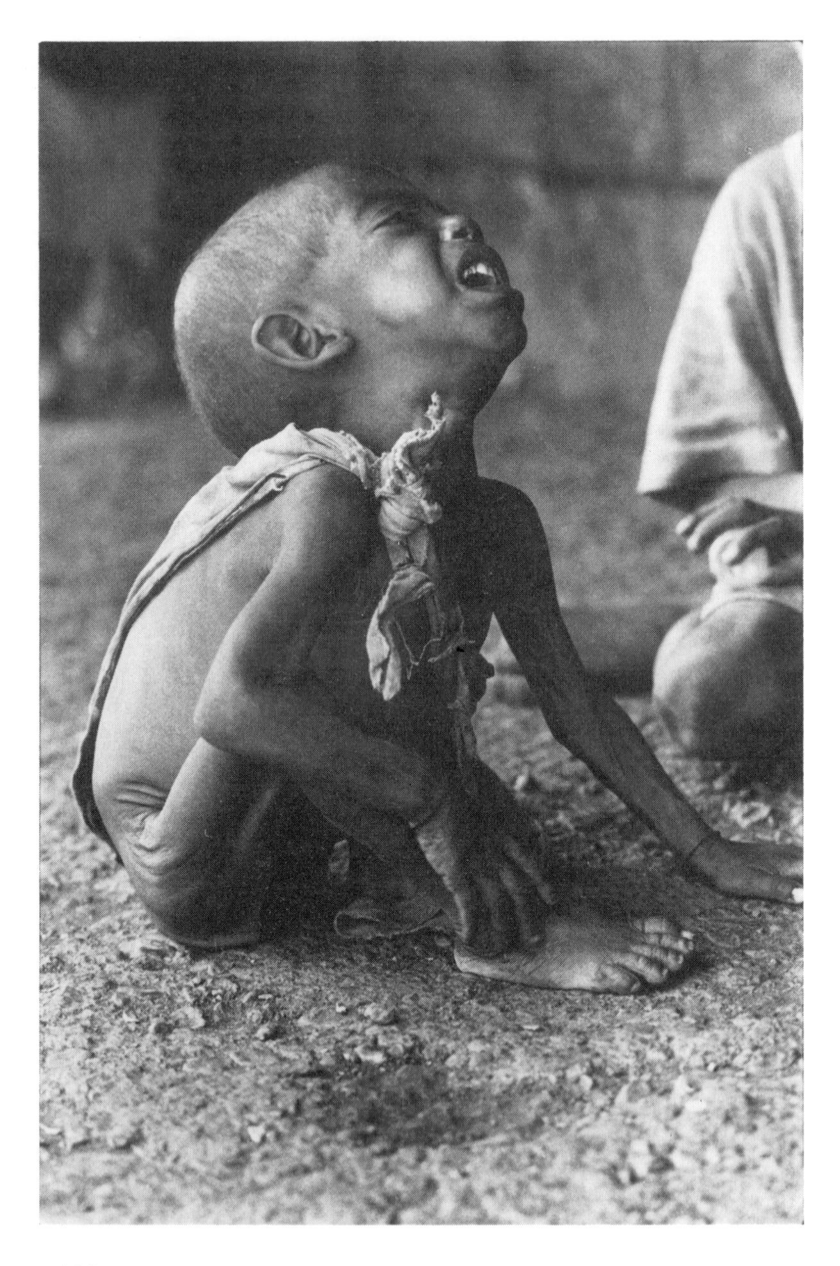

Anguish: a human response to natural disaster after the earthquake hits San Francisco. 1989

Facing page
Cry of despair: the suffering of this Ethiopian child pricked the conscience of the world, sparking Bob Geldof's Live Aid campaign. 1984

Activities

Eyewitnesses: Disasters and War

Background notes

This section focuses on firsthand accounts of events. The pieces are grouped together around two themes – Disasters and War. The disasters include the first eruption of Mount Vesuvius, in 79AD, and two major shipping accidents. The first of these is the explosion on the 19,000 ton *Great Eastern* steamship which, in 1859, was the largest ship in the world. The second disaster is the destruction of the 'unsinkable' *Titanic* in 1912.

The war accounts begin in 1815 at the Battle of Waterloo in which Napoleon's French army was finally defeated. This is the terror of the battlefield at firsthand. The focus then changes to World War II and writers' perceptions of the great Blitz of 1941. The search for a scientific method of recording everyday people's reactions to everyday events had been established by the Mass-Observation movement in 1938. Their methods – collecting data and keeping diaries – provoke vivid accounts of the heavy bombing of Britain's industrial cities. A kind of fascination mixes with the horror. The section ends with an account of perhaps the War's most horrifying event – the nuclear bombing of Hiroshima, Japan, which killed 70,000–80,000 people and injured more than 70,000 others.

The Eruption of Vesuvius

Pair work

1 This eyewitness account was written over 1900 years ago. Using two columns, make a list of the details which make it feel like a historical event and the details which make it feel as if it happened yesterday. Which column has more points? What does this suggest?

2 Which of these words best describes Pliny's tone: *calm*, *fascinated*, *worried*, *objective*, *involved*, *angry*? Explain your choice.

3 Create a role play in which a modern-day TV reporter asks Pliny to tell viewers what he has witnessed. It should include precise details from the written account.

Written assignment

Write up your role play as a TV news script. It might start with the news headlines read by the studio-based newscaster, who then hands over to the reporter in Italy for the interview. Time on television is limited, so the questions need to be precisely chosen to obtain as much information as possible within a two-minute time slot.

Explosion on Board Brunel's *Great Eastern* Steamship

Group work

1 Read the comments one reader has made on this account, and discuss how far you agree with them:

□ The writer concentrates too much on the unpleasant details of the disaster – it becomes distasteful.

□ The style is surprisingly formal, rather poetic in places, and not at all suited to the subject matter.

□ The account describes what happens well enough – but gives no sense of the agony and suffering.

2 How would this eyewitness account of the disaster differ if written for a newspaper front page? Rewrite the account as if you were writing it as a report for a modern tabloid or broadsheet ('quality') newspaper. First, look closely at the newspaper you would be writing for: how long is the front page lead story, on average? How long are the sentences and paragraphs? How complex is the vocabulary? After writing your version, compare it with others in your group and discuss some of the decisions that were involved – what to cut out, what to reword, the vocabulary and grammar changes that were needed, the level of description included.

Written assignment

Imagine you have been asked to reduce this description to 120 words for publication in a book of eyewitness accounts. You are not allowed to change any of the writer's original words, but you will obviously have to cut out large sections of the passage. Write the 120 word version, and then a paragraph explaining how you approached the task and what the result is like.

The *Titanic*: From a Lifeboat

Pair work

Which of these statements do you most agree with? Place them in rank order (from 'most agree with' to 'least agree with') and find a phrase or sentence from the extract to support each one.

□ The writer is appalled at what she sees, but fascinated.

- □ The writer cannot believe what she is seeing.
- □ The writer shows more emotion than Pliny and Sala.
- □ The writer gives a very clear, calm account.

Written assignment

Compare the style of this account with the two previous writers, explaining which you found:
a) most interesting,
b) most informative,
c) most difficult to follow.
Give specific examples from each one to illustrate your opinions.

Memories of Waterloo

Pair work

1 As you read the extract, make a list of the information we discover about the writer. Then discuss the notes you have made, focusing on the writer's character and his attitude to what he describes.
2 Find a quotation from the extract which illustrates:
a) the writer's attitude,
b) the horror of war,
c) the writer's style of writing.
Compare and discuss your choices.

Written assigment

Write a response to this account of war, discussing what you find interesting about it, what you have learned about methods of warfare and the conditions of the time, and how the language shows that the piece was written in the past. You might contrast it with a modern account of warfare from a newspaper report.

They May be Watching You

Pair work

1 What, according to the article, are the main aims of the Mass-Observation movement?
2 What is the writer's attitude to Mass-Observation:
a) supportive?
b) mostly supportive, but wary?
c) Hostile?
Find a quotation which supports your opinion.

3 What is your opinion of the idea of listening in to other people's conversations, observing their behaviour, writing notes and then publishing reports?

Written assignment

Imagine you are one of the people who has been 'observed' – 'Here, what do you mean by eavesdropping like that?' Write a brief letter of complaint to the organizers of the Mass-Observation movement, explaining your objections and criticizing the invasion of privacy. Choose a particular time and place where you might have been observed and refer to this. Then write a reply from the organizers defending the important 'scientific' value of Mass-Observation.

War Begins at Home

Pair work

1 What signs are there in the diary that the outbreak of war was already being prepared for?
2 Describe precisely the writer's attitude to the start of war.
3 Pick out any words or phrases which help to place the extract in historical context.

London Burning

Pair work

1 This writer – a Canadian Sergeant – makes his description vivid by referring to the various senses. As you read, make a list in different columns of the sights, sounds, sensations and smells which he refers to.
2 Pick out any details from the extract which show the writer's fascination for what he sees.

Written assignment

Write the Sergeant's reply to this accusation: 'You seem to see a kind of beauty in the horror of war. Surely you should concentrate on the ugliness.' Write your response as a letter addressed to a relative of one of the victims of the Blitz.

The House Fell About our Ears

Pair work

How does this eyewitness account of the Blitz, by a Nottingham mother, compare with the previous one? Look in particular at the writer's attitude to what she describes.

Written assignment

The writer says little about her emotions when she sees that 'All the upstairs of our house was gone . . .' Imagine how she would have felt and write a detailed personal account in the form of a diary extract.

Visiting Hiroshima

Pair work

1 Pick out any sentences in the extract which show the writer's emotions.

2 Which of these words and phrases best describes the style of the extract: *quietly angry*, *calmly objective*, *shocked*, *appalled*, *moved*? Explain your choice by referring to the text.

Written assignment

Which of the war extracts do you find most powerful? Write about your response to it, explaining your feelings about:

a) the event which is described,

b) the way the writer has conveyed it.

Journalism and Journalists

Background notes

This section looks at the work of journalists and the way their work affects their lives. John Diamond outlines the most important requirements for writing an attention-grabbing newspaper article. Use this to judge later extracts. One of the world's most dedicated newspaper collectors, John Frost gives some of the historical background to the newspaper industry, conveying the excitement it generates for those working within it. Then some newspaper accounts of stories already encountered in the Eyewitness section: these two *Observer* reports, one of a disaster, the other of the effects of war, should give some interesting insights into the differences between first-hand accounts and print journalism.

The focus then moves to newspaper people. Don McCullin is an award winning photojournalist. The extract from his autobiography, *Unreasonable Behaviour*, tells of how he became involved. His first published photograph is also reprinted in this book. Kate Adie, the BBC's Special Assignment reporter, talks to school students about the work of a journalist. We then turn to the work of one of her colleagues, John Simpson, the BBC's Foreign Affairs Editor, on location in Peru.

The extract is a transcript of an investigation into the activities of a guerilla group dealing in drugs

Give me Copy, Fast

Pair work

1 John Diamond is giving advice to features writers. Which of his points do you think, if any, would *not* apply to the news reporters working for a newspaper? How would the advice differ for news reporters in television or radio?
2 Pick two newspaper feature articles at random. Read them through individually, deciding how well they fulfil the requirements outlined by John Diamond. Then swap and read the other one. Finally, discuss how far you both agree in your assessment of the articles.

Written assignment

Take John Diamond's challenge: write a feature article based upon the idea 'Saturday Night with . . .' using his guidelines. The finished piece may be between 500 and 1000 words, giving you more flexibility than an editor would.

Newspaper History

Group work

1 John Frost's article begins by looking back to news events which have remained in his memory. In your group, make a list of the news stories which have made a strong impression on you. How far back does your memory take you? What kind of news stories are they: disasters, celebrations, national, local, etc? Why do you think that these stories have lodged in your memory?
2 Take a look at a selection of newspapers from a single day. Compare their front pages. Are there any stories there which you think will be remembered in the future? How do tabloids and broadsheets (sometimes called 'quality newspapers') differ in their choice of front page lead stories? Are stories based on ideas or personalities in the different papers? Can you see any stories which John Frost might describe as a 'controversy created by a newspaper; a piece of history that will not be found in history books . . .?

Written assignment

John Frost says that newspapers 'provide *real* colour through their styles, language, pictures, of what it was like to be there.' Examine two newspaper stories based on the same event, or choose two of the articles in this book which examine a similar theme. Read them critically looking at the way their style, language and layout inform you about the issue. For example, is the style *clear*, *direct*, *complex*, *confusing*, *patronizing*, *biased*, *objective*? What have you learnt by the end of the story that you didn't previously know? What questions do you have which remain unanswered? Write a detailed comparison of the two stories.

The *Titanic*/The New World: Freedom or Terror

Pair work

1 Read these two newspaper reports from *The Observer*. Both refer to events which were described by eyewitnesses in the first section of this book. Focus on one of the newspaper stories and consider these questions.

□ How does it differ from the eyewitness account in its structure, vocabulary and sense of audience?

□ What information or perspective does it contain which an eyewitness account could not?

□ What qualities does it lack which the eyewitness account has?

Written assignment

Rewrite one of the newspaper articles so that it contains parts of the eyewitness accounts, as if the reporter had interviewed the eyewitness. Aim to achieve a sense of 'what it was like to be there' whilst still including the wider details of the event which only a journalist could give.

Unreasonable Behaviour

Pair work

1 Some critics might accuse McCullin in this extract of glorifying violence. Others might defend him by saying that he reflects life as it really is. Prepare questions you would put to McCullin on a chat show, based on the portrayal of violence. Then role play the interview.

2 Look at the photographs on pages 122–7. What can you tell from them about the time and place in which they were taken? What emotions do they convey? Think up some headlines which might accompany them, for both tabloid and broadsheet newspapers. Then choose one of photos and write an account of your reasons for your choice of headlines. For further discussion of the function of photojournalism, see the article by The Weasel on pages 105–6.

An Interview with Kate Adie

Pair work

1 Read the interview through, making a list of any statements Kate Adie makes which you:
a) strongly agree with,
b) strongly disagree with.
2 Kate Adie makes the point that there is less bias in television/radio reporting than in newspaper coverage. Look again at her reasons for this statement. Then undertake a test of her remark. Video or record two of this evening's news bulletins on television or radio (choose different channels) and pick out one story that seems most likely to contain bias (in particular, a political story). Tomorrow bring in a number of different newspapers and compare their coverage of the story you watched or listened to on the news. Make a detailed comparison, looking for evidence of bias in language, viewpoint and in what has been cut. Feed your findings back to the rest of the class.

Written assignment

As an alternative to the previous assignment, watch one of this evening's main news bulletins. Make a list of the five main stories and time the number of minutes devoted to each one. Then, tomorrow morning, look at a tabloid and broadsheet newspaper and compare their selection of stories and the number of column inches they devote to the story. Are there any surprises in the coverage? Which version of the story is:
a) most informative?
b) most entertaining?
c) most detailed?
d) most authoritative?
e) leaves most questions unanswered?
What does this suggest about the different media's values and audiences?

Following the Shining Path

Pair work

1 This is a copy of the script used on the BBC Nine O'Clock News in which John Simpson reports from Peru. Start by reading it through on your own but discuss any parts which you can't follow with your partner.

2 Simpson's report lasted two minutes 42 seconds when broadcast. Read it through again, aloud, timing how long it takes you. Then work out what kind of images you would choose to show during the report (e.g. footage of specific events or the reporter talking direct to camera), where the commentary should pause, and how long each pause should last. Compare your finished script with others in the group.

3 Simpson has a short amount of time to cover a complex issue. How successful do you find his report in:

a) informing?

b) holding your interest?

c) clarifying issues?

Written assignment

Take a newspaper story from the front page of a recent edition. How would you present this on television news? What would the 30-second introduction by the newsreader say? What would the two-minute film report say? What visuals would accompany the report? Script a two-and-a-half minute television news story for the national news.

The New Journalism: Law and Lawlessness

Background notes

The New Journalism is a term which was invented to describe a mode of reporting which became influential from the 1960s, though in fact it can also be seen in the novels of realistic writers like Dickens and the French novelist Balzac. Tom Wolfe's piece, from his anthology *The New Journalism*, attempts to define four precise techniques which combine to create the genre. Most important, perhaps, is that the writer's role has changed, taking a somewhat different role in the telling of a story, creating mood and dialogue rather as a novelist might.

The examples which follow show how different writers use these techniques to develop stories based on law and lawlessness (William Leith's article in fact does not fit into this category: it is simply an interesting example of a style of reporting). James Mills' piece recreates the life of an American detective: it could almost have been lifted from the pages of Raymond Chandler's fiction. What, then, makes it journalism? Similarly, P. J. O'Rourke's aggressive style and Bill Buford's more inquisitive mode draw on techniques not always associated with journalism. William Leith's piece uses conversation rather than conventional description to convey atmosphere.

The New Journalism

Pair work

1 For clarity, list the four techniques which Wolfe says define the New Journalism. Discuss what you understand by these techniques.
2 Choose one of the extracts in this section and look closely at the way it has been written, paying particular attention to the technique mentioned by Tom Wolfe. What is the effect of the article? Does the style add to its overall power? Are there any disadvantages to such a style?

The Detective

Pair work

1 Which of these words best describes the character of Barrett: *tough, aggressive, loutish, concerned, knowledgeable*? Explain your choice.
2 Make a list of ways in which this piece of reporting is similar and different from what you would expect from a newspaper report.

Written assignment

Interview someone about their job, and then write it up in a dramatic style using dialogue and gritty realism. Try to give a sense of place as well as character.

In Search of the Cocaine Pirates

Pair work

1 Make a list of the words you come across in P. J. O'Rourke's article which you don't understand. Divide them into two catagories:
a) unfamiliar words,
b) slang.
(You can check which is which, if you aren't sure, by looking them up in the dictionary. The slang words probably won't be listed.) Discuss the effect of the vocabulary in the extract.
2 What are the main facts of the article? How would you respond to this critic?

> 'O'Rourke does his best to make a small number of facts lively and interesting. But we learn more about him than we do about the cocaine pirates. There isn't enough substance to the article.'

Written assignment

Write the article as a more conventional 150-word headline story for a tabloid newspaper. Start, perhaps, with the headline; then kick off the story with an attention-grabbing topic sentence, followed by a series of single sentence paragraphs as the story develops. Compare your version with O'Rourke's original.

Among the Thugs

Pair work

1 How does Bill Buford build up the atmosphere of the event he is describing? Look closely at the details he chooses to include.

2 The extract contains observations and reflection. For example, he describes what he *observes* happening on the train. But he also *reflects* on the causes of the "thugs'" behaviour. Discuss how successful you think the mixture of two modes is.

Written assignment

Imagine the man in the first-class carriage as an eyewitness. How would his account of the journey differ from Bill Buford's? How would the supporter's version be different? Write these two versions of events side-by-side.

What you Get when you Cross a Chicken with a Rottweiler

Pair work

1 What does the headline lead you to expect the article to be about?

2 Read it through and then convert it into a role play, continuing where Leith leaves off by actually doing the interview.

Written assignment

Write up the interview that might occur between Leith and the dog breeder. Have a go at imitating the style of William Leith's original piece.

Special Assignment: Death Row

Background notes

This section aims to draw together the different forms of reportage presented so far, and to focus upon a single experience: facing death. The section opens with two early accounts of executions. The first, from 1793, describes *The Observer* newspaper's report of Queen Marie Antoinette's beheading. The second, from almost a century later, describes the refusal of authorities to grant a murderer's last request –

to smoke some tobacco. Also reprinted is an *Observer* editorial questioning the ethics of reporting executions.

These ethics remain topical. One prisoner who gained international attention was Edward Johnson. He was the subject of a Paul Hamann documentary on BBC television in which his final 14 days of life were recorded. The programme shocked the world in 1987. The script from the documentary's opening sequence and examples of the television reviews which followed are included. Two newspaper extracts are also included. The first is an editorial from *Endeavor*, the Death Row newspaper from Huntsville, Texas. The second, a newspaper account, from the *Independent on Sunday*, of an execution in 1992 reminds us that such things continue to happen. Finally, to conclude the section some more first-hand accounts of life on Death Row: two letters describing the conditions are reprinted from Jan Arriens' fascinating and moving book, *Welcome to Hell.*

Execution of the Queen of France

Pair work

1 The account is taken from a newspaper. Can you find any clues that it is a journalist's report rather than another eyewitness account?
2 What do you think is the writer's attitude to the Queen?
3 Find evidence in the language of the article to show that it was written in the past.

Written assignment

Rewrite the report as if you were part of the crowd, eager for the death of the Queen. Which words and sentences require drastic rewriting?

Denial of Tobacco Before Hanging

Group work

1 Organize a role play in your group in which different characters argue for and against granting the prisoner his last request. What are the different arguments which might be used?
2 Pick out all the words and phrases which suggest that the writer is sympathetic to the condemned man. Then discuss in your group how this newspaper report seems:
a) like a factual newspaper report,
b) more like a subjective, eyewitness account.
Provide evidence from the passage in support of each point.

Written assignment

The headline of the article might not be considered 'snappy' enough for a tabloid newspaper. How would a newspaper like *The Sun* or *The Daily Mirror* report this story. Write a front page story of 150 words, paying attention to:

a) headline,
b) one-sentence paragraphs,
c) straightforward vocabulary,
d) eye-catching subheadings,
e) use of labels (e.g. 'hard-hearted Governor').

Rights of the Press at Executions

Written assignment

Write a brief essay stating what you think the rights of the press should be regarding executions. Use these points to help you.

□ Should reporters be allowed to witness a prisoner's death?
□ What are the arguments for and against this?
□ What rights to privacy should a condemned person have?
□ What rights have the public who might want to know the details of the execution?

For a discussion of the rights of the Press at a modern-day execution, read *Plop, Plop, Fizz, Fizz* on pages 86–90.

Fourteen Days in May

Group work

1 Read the script aloud. You will need to double up parts to cover the following voices:

□ Script narrator (reading camera shots on left-hand side),
□ Radio station announcer,
□ Jeff Facelly,
□ Inmates 1 and 2, other Inmates,
□ Narrator,
□ Don Cabana (prison superintendent).

2 Discuss what this opening to the documentary might look like. What is the producer, Paul Hamann, aiming to show in this opening sequence? Why do you think he has not included Johnson himself speaking yet? What signs are there that the documentary will or will not be completely detached from events?

Written assignment

1 Watch the opening sequence of the documentary on video. How does it differ from your impression based upon the script alone? How are your answers to the questions in number 2 (above) different when based on the documentary rather than the script? Write a report describing your response.

2 Write about the main differences you notice between the layout and language of the TV documentary format and a newspaper or magazine article. What does the documentary mode allow the producer to include which the writer would have to cut? What are the advantages, disadvantages, challenges and problems of the different modes of reporting?

TV Reviews: When the Law... / Chronicle of a Death

Pair work

1 What are the main points Antonia Swinson makes about *Fourteen Days in May*? What are the main points Thomas Sutcliffe makes?

2 Pick out one sentence from each review which illustrates the reviewers' overall attitude to the documentary.

3 How do the newspaper styles differ in both reviews? Look in particular at:

a) the type of vocabulary,

b) the length of sentences and paragraphs,

c) the layout of articles,

d) the type of information included in the reviews.

Written assignment

Write a comparison of the two reviews based upon your research above. What can you tell about the different audiences of the two newspapers from the style and layout of the reviews?

I Live on Death Row

Pair work

1 What do you consider to be the main point that Michael Sharpe is making in his article?

2 What image does his writing give of him as a person? Give examples from the text to support your points.

3 Role play an interview in which one person talks to Michael Sharpe about the conditions on Death Row.

Written assignment
'I know that most people will respond by saying that we deserve what we get . . .' Imagine you are one of these people. Write a reply to Michael Sharpe's article in which you defend the system he criticizes.

Plop, Plop, Fizz Fizz

Pair work
1 Make a list of the facts about capital punishment which you learn from the article. Discuss any points which have changed or reinforced your attitudes to the death penalty.
2 Discuss how much you consider the article to be made up of factual reporting and how much contains personal involvement by the reporters. Express your conclusion as a ratio – for example, 60:40 – and compare it with others in the class.

Group work
Organize a debate in your group based on this motion: 'The death penalty can never be justified as a form of punishment.' Those arguing both for and against the motion might include some of the details from pieces in this section to support their arguments.

Written assignment
Write a discursive assignment outlining the arguments for and against the death penalty. Include as many facts as you can, as well as the opinions of prisoners and eyewitnesses included here. Conclude your essay by stating your own opinion.

Welcome to Hell

Pair work
1 What impression do you get of the two writers of these letters?
2 How do the two letters differ – in content and language? Pick out words and phrases which illustrate the differences you notice.

Written assignment
Imagine you had received one of these two letters. How would you reply? What would you want to say? Attempt to write one of these difficult and sensitive replies.

Media Issues

Background notes

This section examines some of the controversies surrounding the media. It begins with the dilemma faced by newspaper owners: whether their main responsibility is to make money or to report the truth, and what if those two aims conflict? Arthur Miller's version of Henrik Ibsen's play *An Enemy of the People* deals with this issue. The rest of the section looks at the power of the media to generate public sympathy as well as to do harm. Bob Geldof, in this extract from his autobiography, *It That It?*, recalls his reactions to the television coverage of mass starvation in Ethiopia. Peggy Noonan's speech for former US President Ronald Reagan tries to come to terms with the television pictures of the space shuttle *Challenger* exploding shortly after takeoff. This event was witnessed live by millions of viewers in America and across the world.

Media coverage of wars and disasters – a recurring concern of this book – is highlighted in The Weasel's reply to a letter of complaint from a reader of *The Independent Magazine*: she objects to the publication of graphic photographs of war. The Weasel, a weekly columnist in *The Independent Magazine*, replies. The ethics of reporting are then the main focus with primary school children writing to express their anger at the portrayal of women on Page 3 of *The Sun*. The final extracts consider how tabloid and broadsheet journalism can offend when it covers sensitive stories in insensitive ways. At other times, as Henry Porter reminds us, the tabloids can simply retreat from the major issues of the day to revel in stories which are just downright silly!

An Enemy of the People

Group work

1 Read the extract aloud in your group. Then discuss how the writer builds up tension and how a simple issue of right and wrong becomes increasingly complex as different characters employ different arguments.

2 Consider the main issue here: Dr Stockmann wishes to reveal that the town springs risk killing bathers. He argues that they must be closed down and repaired. His brother knows that this will take two years, that the town will lose its tourist trade, and that taxes would have to be raised. He argues that the newspaper should keep the issue quiet.

Continue the debate, in role, perhaps asking the rest of the class to watch and then to vote on which side of the argument they support.

Written assignment

What do you consider the main purpose of a newspaper to be? Make a list of six to ten different functions (e.g. for inform, to persuade, to entertain, etc.) and then put them in rank order. Now consider local newspapers.
Would your rank order be any different for them? Using a national and local newspaper published on the same day, write a comparison of the two front pages, using your list of priorities to provide an essay structure.

Is That It?

Pair work

1 Which of these words do you think best describes Bob Geldof's attitude to the news report he watches: *appalled*, *disturbed*, *upset*, *angry*, *sad*? Explain your choice.
2 Pick out one sentence which you think best represents Bob Geldof's attitude to what he has seen.

Group work

1 Reading Geldof's description of the camera wandering 'like a mesmerized observer,' someone might make a statement like this:

> 'The media here was using other people's suffering for our entertainment. The camera crew watched described, and sent their report back – but then *did* nothing.'

First, discuss whether you think this is a fair criticism. Then arrange a small studio discussion programme in which each of you takes on one of the following roles:

- □ media critic,
- □ media defender,
- □ chairperson,
- □ representative of the Ethiopian people themselves.

Use the discussion to air some of the issues about media intrusion at times of disaster, and look again at Kate Adie's comments on the role of newspapers in reporting distressing events, (p. 43–50).

Written assignment

1 Write a defence or criticism of the role of the media in covering a specific news story. Choose three or four precise examples, quoting them as much as possible, and then state your own opinions about their

coverage. Use your conclusion to set out some guidelines to journalists. You might consider the media's response to:
a) disasters,
b) the Royal Family,
c) education.
2 Write about a news story which has moved or disturbed you. Focus, like Bob Geldof, on the first impression the report made, describing it in detail. Then describe how your feelings changed or developed.

The Challenger Disaster

Pair work

1 Peggy Noonan's speech for Ronald Reagan seems to contain a mixture of styles and moods. For each of the words listed below, try to find one example of a word or phrase from the speech:
□ patriotic
□ emotional
□ formal
□ informal
□ poetic.
Then compare the examples you found.
2 Which parts of the speech do you think most powerful? Are there any parts which you dislike? Explain why.
3 Discuss whether you agree with the views of this critic:

> 'This is undoubtedly a great speech, using history and repetition for powerful emotional effect. But the problem is that it *feels* like a speech – it is too full of abstract words like "tragedy", "proud", "grace" and "spirit". The speech would have been more effective if it had been more personal, referring to the astronauts who were killed more specifically.'

Written assignment

Peggy Noonan's speech for Ronald Reagan reacts to a disaster quite differently from Bob Geldof's style of writing. Based on the facts in Geldof's article, try to write a three-minute speech to persuade people that (in Geldof's words) this was 'an international scandal' in which everybody was involved. Write the speech personally, as if you have responded again to those pictures from Ethiopia, but move on to suggest how other people could respond. As a starting point you might use this sentence: 'Today I, and the rest of the world, watched an international disaster which can no longer be ignored...'

Up and Down the City Road

Pair work

1 What are the arguments given in the article for and against publishing graphic war photographs? What other arguments, on either side, can you think of?
2 Discuss your own points of view on this sensitive issue.

Written assignment

Imagine what Mrs Booker's original letter would have said, placing together the evidence from the Weasel's response. Write either that letter, or the one she might wish to write after reading the Weasel's defence of publishing the photos. Start by gathering together reasons for *not* publishing horrific war photographs, however 'beautiful' some might find them.

Page 3 Letters

Group work

1 Read through all the letters and then discuss them: how satisfied would you be with the replies the adults give to the primary school children?
2 Make a list, from the letters and from discussion, of the case for and against Page 3 pictures.
3 What would you reply to these statements?
□ If the models want to pose topless on Page 3, that's their choice.
□ The newspapers only use these photographs to sell more copies – women are therefore being used.
□ Paul Buttle's claim that the 'girls' are 'greatly respected for their beauty' is irrelevant to the argument.
4 Organize a debate in which everyone has to toss a coin to decide which side they are on. Heads should argue in favour of Page 3; tails, argue against. Spend 15 minutes preparing the case, using the letters and your notes.

Written assignment

Write a letter back to *The Sun*, replying to Paul Buttle's defence and making the case against Page 3 photographs.

Hillsborough

Pair work

1 What, according to the extract, are the facts of the Hillsborough disaster?
2 Pick out two or three quotations which you think show the attitude of the writers to *The Sun*. Explain why you chose them.
3 Discuss how you think the newspapers ought to have covered this event. What form of reporting would you define as responsible?

Written assignment

Write about media coverage of disasters, using some of the extracts included in this anthology. Which pieces are most informative? Which seem too involved in the details of the events? How do eyewitnesses' accounts compare with reporters' versions of events – in content and style?

Close Encounters with the Truth

Group work

1 After reading Henry Porter's article on UFOs, discuss these statements, saying whether you agree or disagree with them:
□ *The News of the World* was simply having a bit of fun. Porter takes it too seriously.
□ Porter accepts, at the end of his article, that it's all a hoax. It's the editor – Derek Jameson – who is taken in by it.
□ Although funny, the appearance of the UFO articles means that more serious stories have been left out of the paper. That is not amusing.
2 Take *The News of the World* UFO story and convert it into a news bulletin report. One person should play the role of the newsreader; another the on the spot reporter in Suffolk; two others the eyewitnesses. Rehearse and then present your bulletin to the rest of the class.

Written assignment

Choose an improbable story – UFO landings in school playground, for example – and write a tabloid style newspaper story. Remember to refer to John Diamond's guidance on writing, so that your style is snappy and attention-grabbing.

Extended Activities

1 Organize a discussion on one or more of these issues:

□ Television news informs; broadsheets bore; tabloids trivialize.

□ The role of a reporter is to hold our interest as much as to inform us.

□ There is no such job as 'reporter': the role differs according to each medium.

2 Have a debate in which you consider the idea that eyewitnesses' reports are usually more revealing than any other form of reportage. Use specific examples from this book to support your viewpoint.

3 Discuss and then write about the idea that too much reportage generally – and too much in this book – is written by men for men.

4 Discuss and write about the idea that there should be limits to the kinds of methods journalists should use – for example, phone-tapping, powerful camera lenses, and 'door-stepping' techniques should be outlawed.

5 What, in your opinion, are the main requirements of a good journalist? Make a list of features, and then write an essay explaining your point of view. Illustrate it with examples of good and bad practice where possible.

6 Write a detailed eyewitness account of an event you have seen during the past few days, however trivial it seems. How would your account differ if it were being written for publication?

7 Read some of the New Journalism included in this anthology. Write a response to the content (is it always aggressive?) and the style (does it trivialize the subject by treating it as a novel might?), giving specific examples from your reading.

8 How have newspaper reporting styles changed over the years? Look at some of the examples in this book of pre-twentieth century newspaper stories and compare them with stories on similar themes from this week's newspapers. Consider how layout, news values and language have developed.

9 Look back at the section called Special Assignment: Death Row. Write about how the different articles affected you, which you found most interesting or disturbing, and what you learnt overall from the various pieces. Have these changed your opinion at all on the existence of the death penalty?

Wider Reading

Assignments

1 Read some more eyewitness accounts from the books suggested in the booklist. Which ones feel dated and which seem relevant and fresh today? Explore the qualities needed to keep such accounts interesting.
2 Read some of the New Journalism titles given in the booklist, for example Truman Capote's *Music for Chameleons*. Write about the styles such writers use and where you think the boundary is between fact and fiction.
3 Choose some of the texts which contain war reminiscences from different periods. Look also at some anthologies of poetry and prose on the same theme. How do fictional and non-fictional books differ in their response to war?
4 Read one or more of the novels about media life, or a biography of a journalist. Write about what you learn about their work and the way of life that accompanies it.
5 Look at some books of news photographs and write a personal response structured around five photographs, explaining what photography can convey in a news story which words cannot.

Booklist

Eyewitnesses

The following anthologies contain a feast of firsthand accounts:
Ronald Blythe ed., *The Penguin Book of Diaries*, Penguin, 1991
John Carey ed., *The Faber Book of Reportage*, Faber, 1987
Philip Kerr ed., *The Penguin Book of Lies*, Penguin, 1990
Felix Pryor ed., *The Faber Book of Letters*, Faber, 1988
Godfrey Smith ed., *How It Was in The War*, Pavillion, 1989

Also recommended:
Jan Arriens, *Messages from Hell*, Ian Faulkner Publishing, 1991
Janina Baumann, *Winter in the Morning: A Young Girl's Life in the Warsaw Ghetto and Beyond*, Virago, 1991
Vera Brittain, *Diary 1939–45*, Gollanz, 1981
Angus Calder and Dorothy Sheridan, *Speak for Yourself: A Mass-Observation Anthology (1937–49)*, Jonathan Cape, 1984
St Jean de Crevecoeur, *Letters from an American Farmer*, Penguin, 1982

Maria Edgeworth, *Letters from England*, OUP, 1971
Anne Frank, *The Diary of Anne Frank*, Pan, 1968
Joyce Grenfell, *The Time of My Life: Entertaining the Troops*, Coronet, 1990
Samuel Peyps, *The Shorter Pepys*, Bell and Hyman, 1985
Dorothy Wordsworth, *Journals*, OUP, 1993 (The illustrated edition is the most interesting.)

Journalism and Journalists

A Day in the Life of America [photography] eds. Rick Smolan and David Cohen, Collins, 1986
Joanna Anstey and John Silverlight, *The Observer Observed*, Barrie & Jenkins, 1991
Robert Fisk, *Pity the Nation*, OUP, 1991
Clive James, *Falling Towards England*, Jonathan Cape, 1985
Glyn Jones ed., *The Giant Book of True Crime*, Magpie Books, 1992
Robert Kee ed., *The Picture Post Album*, (photography) Barrie & Jenkins, 1989
Brian Lake, *British Newspapers: A History and Guide for Collectors*, Shepperd Press, 1984
Don McCullin, *Unreasonable Behaviour*, Jonathan Cape, 1990
Lorraine Monk, *Photographs That Changed the World*, Doubleday, 1989
John Simpson, *Despatches from the Barricades*, Hutchinson, 1990
The Quake of '89 (photography), Chronicle Books, 1989
The New Yorker Book of War Pieces, Bloomsbury, 1990

The New Journalism

Bill Buford, *Among the Thugs*, Secker & Warburg, 1991
Bill Buford ed., *Granta 25: The Murderee*, Granta Books, 1988
Bill Buford ed., *Granta 29: New World*, Granta Books, 1989
Truman Capote, *Music for Chameleons*, Picador, 1981
Spalding Gray, *Swimming to Cambodia*, Picador, 1987
Michael Herr, *Despatches*, Picador, 1978
P. J. O'Rourke, *Republican Party Reptile*, Picador, 1987
Hunter S. Thompson, *Fear and Loathing in Las Vegas*, Paladin, 1972
Tom Wolfe, *The New Journalism*, Picador, 1990

Media Issues

Peter Chippendale and Chris Horrie, *Stick it up your Punter!: The Fall and Rise of the Sun*, Mandarin, 1992
Bob Geldof, *Is That It?*, Penguin, 1986
S. J. Taylor, *Shock Horror!*, Corgi, 1992
Janice Winship, *Inside Women's Magazines*, Pandora, 1987

Fiction

Noel Barber, *A Woman of Cairo*, Coronet, 1984
George Gissing, *New Grub Street*, Penguin, 1968
Joseph Heller, *Catch 22*, Jonathan Cape, 1993
Ernest Hemingway, *A Farewll to Arms*, Jonathan Cape, 1992
Erich Maria Remarque, *All Quiet on the Western Front*, Picador Classics, 1987
William Thackeray, *Pendennis, The History of*, Penguin Classics, 1972
Evelyn Waugh, *Scoop*, Penguin, 1990